What Children Need to Learn to READ

The complete parent's guide to ensuring literacy, a love of reading, and school readiness

Birth through the Early Grades Edition

Michelle Vallene

Learners Lane

www.LearnersLane.com

What Children Need to Learn to READ

The complete parent's guide to ensuring literacy, a love of reading, and school readiness

Birth through the Early Grades Edition

Michelle Vallene

PO Box 2303, Redmond, WA 98073
Website: www.LearnersLane.com
Email: info@LearnersLane.com

For information about special discounts for bulk purchases,
please contact us at info@LearnersLane.com.

Publisher's Cataloging-in-Publication

Vallene, Michelle.

What Children Need to Learn to READ: The complete parent's guide to ensuring literacy, a love of reading, and school readiness. Birth through the Early Grades Edition / Michelle Vallene.

p. cm.

Includes index.

ISBN 978-0-9822856-0-2

Credits

www.kleineedit.com
www.knockoutbooks.com

www.writingandediting.biz
www.writetoyourmarket.com

Edited by Walter Kleine, Kleine Editorial Service and Robin Quinn, Quinn's Word for Word
Book cover and interior designed by Peri Poloni-Gabriel, Knockout Design
Cover text written by Graham Van Dixhorn, Write To Your Market, Inc.
Author photo by David Randall

Visit our website: www.LearnersLane.com. Email: info@LearnersLane.com.

Dedication

★ ★ ★

*This book is dedicated to my dear friend,
Suzie Connor, who shares my vision of
helping children to love learning.
Thank you for being with me every
step of the way!*

Acknowledgments

 would like to thank my loving husband, Brian, who has supported me in making my dreams a reality.

Thanks also goes out to my wonderful children, Briana, Brittany, and Kevin, who have been my life and my inspiration. Thank you for all that you have taught me along my parenting journey. I am so proud of the extraordinary people that you have grown to become.

Thanks to my parents, Mary and Charles Moshier, for believing in me and giving me all the love and support that I needed to become who I am today.

In addition, thanks goes to my sister, Marianne, who, with her excellent writing skills, helped me with the early revisions of this book.

I would also like to thank my first employer and friend, Janet Bequette, for all of the opportunities that she gave me and for all that she taught me about children.

Thanks also goes out to Paula Randolph, a Better Schools Reading Teacher, from Redmond Elementary in Redmond, Washington, for taking the time to give us her valuable feedback.

I would like to thank my fastidious editors, Walter Kleine, Kleine Editorial Service, and Robin Quinn, Quinn's Word for Word, for all of their outstanding, detail-oriented work.

A special thank you goes out to Peri Poloni-Gabriel, Knockout Design, for her outstanding cover and interior design layout.

I would also like to thank Graham Van Dixhorn, Write To Your Market, Inc., for his eloquent cover text.

Contents

Chapter 6 — **Music & Songs** . . . 57

Foreword

How different would your life be if you couldn't read or write? I bet the difference would be dramatic. For one thing, you wouldn't be looking at this page of seemingly meaningless characters. For another, you'd be way less connected to and informed about the world around you. And no matter what you were seeking in life, your options would be dramatically limited.

But what about the other end of the spectrum? What if you *could* read and write and communicate with clarity and confidence? You would have the opportunity to connect at a deep level with your community and the world around you. And in doing so, your ability to achieve the life of your dreams would be greatly enhanced.

If you are interested in providing your child with these powerful tools that lead to a lifetime of success, then you are holding the right book in your hands. Michelle Vallene's book *What Children Need to Learn to Read* is the perfect way to start your child's journey to literacy.

The fun and educational activities in this book are a great way to ignite your child's love for reading. Talk about quality time with your child! The activities in this book will enhance your relationship with your child, stimulate their self-confidence, and foster a life-long appreciation for reading and writing.

Have fun!

Derek Munson
Author of the award-winning children's book *Enemy Pie*

What Children Need to Learn to READ

Introduction

Welcome to

What Children Need to Learn to READ

From Birth through the Early Grades

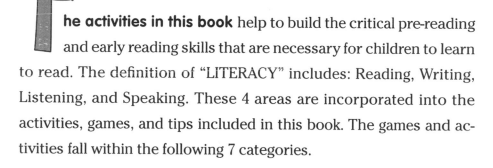

he activities in this book help to build the critical pre-reading and early reading skills that are necessary for children to learn to read. The definition of "LITERACY" includes: Reading, Writing, Listening, and Speaking. These 4 areas are incorporated into the activities, games, and tips included in this book. The games and activities fall within the following 7 categories.

- ✔ Baby and Toddler Games
- ✔ Letters and Their Sounds
- ✔ Sight Words
- ✔ Read Alouds, Listening, and Comprehension
- ✔ Phonics
- ✔ Writing
- ✔ Word Play

We have also included valuable parenting tips, ideas for a reading party and a children's book club, poems, rhymes, songs, and tongue twisters. For your reference, both a children's reading checklist and a parents' checklist are included. These checklists are designed to help you determine what your child is likely to know about reading at different age levels, and offer ideas on how you can help them. At the end of the book are lists of wonderful children's books, magazines, computer games, Internet sites, and parent resources that you can use and refer to again and again.

Your child will be playing games, singing, and rhyming his/her way to a life-long love of reading. This book is the first step toward setting the groundwork for reading mastery and success!

Have Fun and Happy Reading!

We would love to hear from you! Please send us an email at info@LearnersLane.com and give us your feedback. Tell us what you liked best, what you would like to see in future books or editions and any ideas you have for games or activities that we might include in our next edition. We would also love to hear your personal success stories related to the ideas, suggestions, games or activities discussed in *What Children Need to Learn to READ*. You can also send your feedback, ideas, and stories to us by mail at: Learners Lane, P.O. Box 2303, Redmond, WA 98073.

Author's Message

As an elementary school teacher, founder of Learners Lane (offering unique and engaging educational products and services), and a mother of three amazing children, I have seen the challenges we face in bringing up our children to be happy, literate, and productive adults. In my attempt to address the literacy challenge, I have put this book together, combining hard facts and proven educational techniques with fun and interactive games and activities.

I believe that in the clinical debate over the proper way to teach reading, we can lose sight of the real goals of helping children to be successful readers, and of fostering an enjoyment of reading that will last throughout their lifetimes. There is no one correct way to reach these goals. What it takes is a little knowledge and some unforgettable precious time spent with your child.

Have fun with these activities and games, and give your child your attention and lots of positive encouragement. Remember, you want them to enjoy the process and see the excitement of reading in your eyes! Your child will pick up on this and recognize the value that you place on them as an individual, and on the importance of reading!

Michelle Vallene

"When children learn to read,
they have the key that opens the door
to all the knowledge of the world.
Without this key, many children
are left behind."

U.S. Department of Education
Office of Communications and Outreach
Helping Your Child Become a Reader
Washington, D.C. 2005

Chapter 1

Parent/Teacher Tips

As parents and teachers, we are always looking for tips to better prepare our children for the future. We all want the best for our kids. We want them to lead happy and successful lives. In today's information-based world, reading is absolutely essential for success. The following are tips for helping children on the path to reading achievement.

Read to Your Child Every Day

Research has shown reading to your child to be the single most important thing you can do to help him/her build critical reading skills and achieve reading success. Reading to your child helps stimulate early brain development and builds vocabulary, story sequencing, and comprehension. It is also a great bonding time for you and your child. Have fun with this! You can even make up different voices for the characters. (Believe me; your child will love this!)

> "Reading to young children promotes language acquisition and correlates with literacy development and, later on, with achievement in reading comprehension and overall success in school."
>
> U.S. Department of Education (2004)

Reading to your child shows them that:

- ✔ Books are an enjoyable form of entertainment.
- ✔ You can learn new things from books.
- ✔ Words in books are what give them meaning.
- ✔ You value them as a person and enjoy spending time with them.

Babies enjoy hearing your voice. As you read to them, they pick up on the flow of language. When they're very young, it doesn't really matter what you read to them. You can read the newspaper or a novel aloud to them, or even your shopping or to do list. We all love to multi-task.

The best books for babies are colorful and simple. They should have a strong rhythmic pattern, and depict things that your baby may already be familiar with. Books that have texture (such as fabric) or could prompt actions (like clapping, pointing, or finding something) are great. Use different voices and have fun as you read. Your baby will pick up on that and start to see reading as a special bonding time with you. Babies love it when you make silly faces or gestures to keep their attention while reading. Board books, cloth books, and plastic/vinyl books are great, because your baby can hold the book or grab at the pages without ripping or destroying the book. The plastic/vinyl books are also fun for the bath, and bring relief to a teething baby!

Toddlers enjoy simple stories and love to look at pictures. Children will learn that we read a book from front to back, left to right, and top to bottom. They will also learn how to hold a book and how to turn the pages. Don't worry if your child wants you to read the same story over and over again. I know it can get monotonous to us as adults, but children learn through repetition. If they become bored or lose interest in a story, move on to another activity. You can come back to reading at another time. Be flexible!

As you read, ask your child to show you things in the story by pointing at them. ("Where is the dog?" "Where is the red ball?" Etc.) Kids love to find things (it's like a treasure hunt). It helps to keep them engaged in the story and makes it more meaningful to them.

Get out and about with your toddler. This could be in your own yard or neighborhood, or could be a trip to the park, zoo, beach, library or grandma's house, etc. The more experiences that you offer them, the more connections they will be able to make in their learning and in their reading. While you're out, discuss what you're seeing and doing. Ask them open-ended questions (not just yes or no questions), and answer their questions. This will help them to develop a stronger vocabulary and will increase their language skills, which should, in turn, set the stage for future learning.

When your **preschooler or early elementary school child** "pretends" to read their favorite book to you, sit back and enjoy! They're learning to retell the story, with its sequence of beginning, middle, and end. They're also seeing how words go together to make sense. Most of all, they're beginning to see themselves as readers! Praise them for a job well done.

Some children like to draw or wiggle in their seat while they listen to a story. For many children, this helps them focus.

You can have your child predict what will happen in the story before starting the book. Use the title of the book and the illustration on the cover to spark ideas. Stop periodically, and have your child recap what has already occurred in the story and predict what will happen next. Ask your child how the characters might be feeling, and what they would do if they were one of the characters. Have them create a new ending to the story, or draw a picture of the story when you're done reading it. You and your child can act out the story. You don't have to do all these things every time you read to your child. Just sitting down for some quiet cuddle-reading time is so important for your child's sense of family, security, self-esteem, and, of course, the development of reading skills!

As your child learns to read, listen to them and give them lots of encouragement and praise. You can take turns reading different parts of a story. If your child is struggling on a word, you can have them:

- ✔ Use picture clues. (Looking at a picture can help him/her determine what the word is.)

- ✔ Sound it out. (Phonics)

- ✔ Make Sense: Skip the word, finish the sentence, and then see if they can figure out what word would make sense in the missing location. (Context clues)

✔ Say the word for them, to keep the momentum of the story going.

✔ Tell them the word, and help them practice it and memorize it (especially if it is a sight word; a common word in written language that usually cannot be sounded out).

Try to alternate your approaches so that they learn how to use different ways to figure out unknown words. Let them know how proud you are of them and their reading accomplishments!

Have Books around the House and in the Car

One of the best things you can do is to have books accessible to your children wherever they are. Try to have children's books in as many rooms of your house as you can. The more they see the books, the more likely they are to pick them up, look at them, and read them. Having books in the car is a great idea. Switch them out often, to keep them fresh and interesting. If kids get bored in the car, all they have to do is pick up a book.

Give Books or Book Store Gift Cards as Gifts

Books are a great gift for children. It helps them advance their reading skills, and shows them that you value books. If you're not sure which books they already have or which new books they would like to read, a gift card to your local book store is a great idea. That way you can make an event out of taking your child to the book store so that they can look around and choose books for themselves. Your child's personal library of books becomes very special. They will want to read old favorites over and over, and add new books.

Play Reading Games

Play the reading games and activities that are shown in this book. You and your child will have loads of fun, and your child will gain valuable skills in the advancement of his/her reading abilities!

Computer Games to Learn Reading Skills

There are many excellent computer games that help children to learn and work on their reading skills. It's important to offer a variety of options to develop reading skills, and using the computer can be a unique and interesting way to do this.

See Appendices A and B for computer resources that work on beginning reading skills.

Library and Book Store Visits/Story-Time

Most libraries and many local book stores have special story-times that are free to attend. Children have a delightful time listening to a variety of stories, from a variety of different readers. In addition, check out summer reading programs sponsored by libraries, book stores, or toy stores. Take advantage of these great opportunities to encourage a love of books in your children.

Modeling

Parents should model good reading habits themselves. Your child should "catch" you reading books, magazines, newspapers, etc., and see you enjoying and gaining knowledge through printed materials.

MY FIRST
READING
BOOK

What Children Need to Learn to READ

Chapter 2

A Children's Language Accomplishments Checklist (Birth to Age 6)

Help Your Child Become a Reader

earning to read is built on a foundation of language skills that children start to learn at birth, a process that is both complicated and amazing. Most children develop certain skills as they move through the early stages of learning language. By age 7, most children are reading.

The following list of accomplishments is based on current scientific research in the fields of reading, early childhood education, and child development. Studies continue in these fields, and there is still much to learn. As you look over the accomplishments, keep in mind that children vary a great deal in how they develop and learn. If you have questions or concerns about your child's progress, talk with your child's doctor, teacher, or a speech and language therapist. For children with any kind of disability or learning problem, the sooner they can get the special help they need, the easier it will be for them to learn.

From birth to age 3, most babies and toddlers become able to:

- ❑ Make sounds that imitate the tones and rhythms that adults use when talking.

- ❑ Respond to gestures and facial expressions.

- ❑ Begin to associate words they hear frequently with what the words mean.

- ❑ Make cooing, babbling sounds in the crib, which gives way to enjoying rhyming and nonsense word games with a parent or caregiver.

- ❑ Play along in games like "peek-a-boo" and "pat-a-cake."

- ❑ Handle objects like board books and alphabet blocks in their play.

- ❑ Recognize certain books by their covers.

- ❑ Pretend to read books.

- ❑ Understand how books should be handled.

- ❑ Share books with an adult as a routine part of life.

- ❑ Name some objects in a book.

- ❑ Talk about characters in books.

- ❑ Look at pictures in books and realize that they are symbols of real things.

- ❑ Listen to stories.

- ❑ Ask that adults read or write with them.

- ❑ Begin to pay attention to specific aspects of printed language, like the first letters of their names.

- ❑ Scribble with a purpose (trying to write or draw something).

- ❑ Produce some letter-like forms and scribbles that resemble, in some way, writing.

From ages 3-4, most preschoolers become able to:

❏ Enjoy listening to and talking about storybooks.

❏ Understand that print carries a message.

❏ Make attempts to read and write.

❏ Identify familiar signs and labels.

❏ Participate in rhyming games.

❏ Identify some letters and make some letter-sound matches.

❏ Use known letters (or their best attempt to write the letters) to represent written language, especially for meaningful words, like their names, or phrases like "I love you."

At age 5, most kindergartners become able to:

❏ Sound as if they are reading when they pretend to read.

❏ Enjoy being read to.

❏ Retell simple stories.

❏ Use descriptive language to explain or to ask questions.

❏ Recognize letters and letter-sound matches.

❏ Show familiarity with rhyming and beginning sounds.

❏ Understand that print is read left-to-right and top-to-bottom.

❏ Begin to match spoken words with written ones.

❏ Begin to write letters of the alphabet and some words they use and hear often.

❏ Begin to write stories with some readable parts.

At age 6, most first-graders can:

❑ Read and retell familiar stories.

❑ Use a variety of ways to help with reading a story, like rereading, predicting what will happen, asking questions, or using visual cues or pictures.

❑ Decide on their own to use reading and writing for different purposes.

❑ Read some things aloud with ease.

❑ Identify new words by using letter-sound matches, parts of words, and their understanding of the rest of a story or printed item.

❑ Identify an increasing number of words by sight.

❑ Sound out and represent major sounds in a word when trying to spell.

❑ Write about topics that mean a lot to them.

❑ Try to use some punctuation marks and capitalization.

Source:
U.S. Department of Education
Office of Communications and Outreach
Helping Your Child Become a Reader
Washington, D.C., 2005

Chapter 3

A Reading Checklist for Parents

Help Your Child Become a Reader

There are many ways that you can encourage your child to become a reader. Here are some questions that you can ask yourself to make sure that you are keeping on track:

For Babies (6 weeks to 1 year)

- ❏ Do I provide a comfortable place for our story-time? Is my child happy to be in this place?

- ❏ Am I showing my child the pictures in the book? Am I changing the tone of my voice as I read to show emotion and excitement?

- ❏ Am I paying attention to how my child responds? What does she especially like? Is she tired and ready to stop?

For Toddlers (1 to 3 years)

All the questions above, plus:

- ❏ Does my child enjoy the book we are reading?

- ❏ Do I encourage my child to "pretend read," joining in where he has memorized a word or phrase?

- ❏ When I ask questions, am I giving my child enough time to think and answer?

- ❏ Do I tie ideas in the book to things that are familiar to my child? Do I notice if he does this on his own?

- ❏ Do I let my child know how much I like his ideas and encourage him to tell me more?

- ❏ Do I point out letters, such as the first letter of his name?

For Preschoolers (3 and 4 years)

All of the questions above, plus:

- ❏ Do I find ways to help my child begin to identify sounds and letters and to make letter-sound matches?

For Kindergartners (5 years)

All of the questions above, plus:

- ❏ Do I find ways to help my child begin to identify some printed words?

- ❏ Do I let my child retell favorite stories to show that she knows how the story develops and what's in it?

For Beginning First-Graders (6 years)

All of the questions above, plus:

- ❏ Do I give my child the chance to read a story to me using printed words, picture clues, his memory—or any combination of these ways that help him make sense of the story?

Remember: Children learn step-by-step in a process that takes time and patience. They vary a great deal in what holds their interest and in the rate at which they make progress.

Source:
U.S. Department of Education
Office of Communications and Outreach
Helping Your Child Become a Reader
Washington, D.C., 2005

What Children Need to Learn to READ

Chapter 4

Baby & Toddler Games

Interacting **with your baby** will help stimulate his/her brain development. This includes talking, playing, singing, moving, and reading with your baby.

Introducing them to letters and books at an early age will help prepare them for learning to read. The positive experiences that you have with your baby or toddler will help them make learning connections, which will set the stage for later reading success. The time you spend playing with your baby or toddler also conveys to them how much you value and love them. Your child's self-esteem and self-confidence grows through these interactions, which greatly helps in later learning and reading success. Games and activities that include cause and effect, imitation, anticipation, and a back-and-forth exchange, all help your child's brain development and help to build valuable cognitive and pre-reading skills. Have fun and start building the foundation!

BOUNCING BALLOON

What you will need:

✔ Helium balloon

OR

✔ Baby sock with bell attached

What to do:

Loosely tie the ribbon of a helium balloon around your child's ankle. Your child will begin to notice that when she moves her leg, the balloon will move—cause and effect. You can also play this game by attaching a bell to a baby sock and putting it on your child's foot (some socks come with a bell already attached). Activity gyms will also help your child learn that when she does something, something happens (moves). Constant supervision is required with this game.

★★★

TALK TO ME!

What you will need:

✔ Just you and your baby

What to do:

Talk to your baby as much as you can. Narrate everything you do while they're with you. Talk about the toys they're playing with. For example: "That sure made a crinkly sound" or "The clown just popped up." Ask questions about the toys. If your child can't talk yet, you can answer the questions for them. They will be learning many new words, and will start to pick up on the basics of conversational interactions.

★★★

BABY SIGN LANGUAGE

What you will need:

✔ Just you and your baby

What to do:

Make up simple signs that you can do with your hands or body that stand for common things that your child sees, does, or needs. We all use common signs like "thumbs up," which means good job. We nod our heads for yes or no, and we wave goodbye. Even before your child has verbal skills, they can learn to make signs that stand for different words. This helps them communicate more effectively. Studies have shown that they may learn to talk sooner, and they don't seem to get as frustrated about not being able to communicate. They also learn that there are different symbols for objects and words, which they need to learn in order to talk and read. A useful book that explains this in more detail and has many different "baby sign" ideas is *Baby Signs: How to Talk with Your Baby before Your Baby Can Talk* by Linda Acredolo, Ph.D. and Susan Goodwyn, Ph.D.

★ ★ ★

PAT-A-CAKE

What you will need:

✔ Just you and your baby

What to do: (sing or say)

Pat-A-Cake (Pat baby's hands together.)

Pat-A-Cake (Pat baby's hands together.)

Baker's Man

Bake me a cake as fast as you can!

Pat it and roll it (Roll baby's hands over and over.)

And mark it with "B" (Have baby's hand draw out a "B" in the air.)

And put it in the oven for baby and me! (Push baby's hands out.)

★ ★ ★

PEEK-A-BOO

What you will need:

✔ Blanket

What to do:

Hold up a blanket between you and your baby. Drop the blanket down or pop your face up from behind the blanket and say, "Peek-A-Boo!" in a fun and energetic way, with a smile on your face. Then repeat. This should delight your baby into giggle mania!

★ ★ ★

HIDDEN TREASURE

What you will need:

✔ Just you and your child

What to do:

Hide something in one of your hands and have your child guess which hand it is in. Continue this game by following a pattern (right, left, right, left). They will pick up on the pattern and begin to anticipate where you will hide the object the next time. Then change the pattern (right, right, left, left) and see whether your child can re-adjust his thinking to learn the new pattern and guess what comes next again. This is a great game to challenge your child's mind, and also to help them learn about patterns. They will need to understand patterns for both reading and mathematical thinking.

★ ★ ★

BEEP!

What you will need:

✔ Just you and your child

What to do:

Start the game by having your child touch your nose. Each time he touches your nose, make the sound "Beep." He will love feeling like he is in control of the sound. He will see that when he touches your nose, you make a "Beep" sound (cause and effect). You can vary the sound that you make, or jump up a bit when he touches your nose. Then you can have him touch a different area and make a new sound or jump up. This will keep him tuned in, interested, and engaged in problem solving activities.

MAKE THAT ANIMAL SOUND

What you will need:

✔ OPTIONAL: Pictures of animals

What to do:

Name an animal and tell your child what sound that animal makes. Next, ask them to tell you what sound the animal makes. If they can't make the sound yet, you can make the animal sound for them. Your child will soon pick up on how to make each of the sounds, will have great fun making them, and will feel pride in this accomplishment.

Examples of different animals and their sounds:

✔ Dog: "Woof, Woof"

✔ Cat: "Meow, Meow"

✔ Duck: "Quack, Quack"

✔ Cow: "Moo, Moo"

✔ Horse: "Neigh, Neigh"

✔ Pig: "Oink, Oink"

✔ Sheep: "Baa, Baa"

RIDING ON A PONY

What you will need:

✔ Just you and your child

What to do:

Sit on the floor with your legs together, straight out. You might want to lean against a couch or chair. Have your toddler sit on your lap facing out. Hold their arms, hands or waist while playing this game. Bounce your knees up and down while saying:

Riding on a pony
Downtown,
Better watch out or
You might fall down!

When you say "down," move your legs apart and have them gently fall to the floor while you support them for safety. They will begin to anticipate what will happen next, enhancing their cognitive development. Vary the length of time you hold the sounds for the word "fall" (faaaaaall) so they're not quite sure when you will say "down." They will truly delight in the anticipation!

★ ★ ★

SIMON SAYS

What you will need:

✔ Just you and your child

What to do:

Have your child copy what you do by saying, "Simon Says…"

For example: "Simon says put your hands on your head."

"Simon says jump up and down."

"Simon says turn around." Etc.

Then you can reverse roles and have your child be Simon. When you first play the game, always say, "Simon says…" Later, you can transition to the more traditional way of playing the game, where you catch them if they do what you ask, but you haven't said, "Simon says" first.

FOLLOW THE LEADER

What you will need:

✔ Just you and your child

What to do:

Have your child follow you around the house or yard and do what you do. If you hop, they hop. If you walk around a bush, they walk around the bush. If you crawl on your hands and knees, they crawl on their hands and knees. Then have your child be the leader and you follow what they do.

WHAT'S MISSING?

What you will need:

- ✔ Tray or cookie sheet
- ✔ 5 or 6 (or more) objects your child can recognize

What to do:

Place 5 or 6 objects (or more) on a tray or cookie sheet and have your child look and try to remember the objects. Then have them turn around while you remove an object. Ask them to tell you which one is missing. You can also reverse roles and have your child take the object away and have you guess what's missing. This activity helps with early visual discrimination skills, which are important in learning to read.

PRETEND PLAY

What you will need:

- ✔ Just you and your child
- ✔ Optional items include dress-up clothes, kitchen supplies, dolls, toy cars and trucks, blocks, stuffed animals, pretend phones, blankets for forts, etc.

What to do:

Encourage your child to participate in pretend-play activities. As kids play, they usually talk about what they're doing. This helps them develop language skills and vocabulary more quickly. Kids love it when you get right in there and pretend-play with them.

What Children Need to Learn to READ

Chapter 5

Rhyming

Action Poems & Nursery Rhymes

Poems and nursery rhymes help children to listen to the words and hear how language flows. Studies have shown that children's exposure to nursery rhymes helps them with later reading success. New words are easier to learn when they're introduced in rhyme. Learning rhyming words helps children recognize word families like cat, bat, rat, mat, and sat.

When you read a poem or rhyme to your child, stop and let them fill in a missing word or phrase. This will help them predict what comes next and show them how language flows together. Nursery rhymes and poems will help your child develop an ear for language and its flow. Children love to participate in the reading process, and will learn to anticipate what's coming next. This will also help them with their listening skills. You can even substitute your child's name, siblings' names,

> *"Three year olds' exposure to nursery rhymes is directly correlated with later reading success."*
>
>
>
> Study (Maclean, Bryant, and Bradley 1987)

and friends' names for the names of the characters in the nursery rhymes.

Below is an example of a rhyming poem and the words a child could fill in. (Other rhyming poems follow on the subsequent pages.)

MONKEYS ON THE BED

Words for Child to Add:

Five little monkeys jumping on the _____ (bed)
One fell off and bumped his _____ (head)

Poem:

Five little monkeys jumping on the bed
One fell off and bumped his head
Mama called the doctor and the doctor said,
"No more monkeys jumping on the bed!"

Four little monkeys jumping on the bed
One fell off and bumped his head
Mama called the doctor and the doctor said,
"No more monkeys jumping on the bed!"

Three little monkeys jumping on the bed
One fell off and bumped his head
Mama called the doctor and the doctor said,
"No more monkeys jumping on the bed!"

Two little monkeys jumping on the bed
One fell off and bumped his head
Mama called the doctor and the doctor said,
"No more monkeys jumping on the bed!"

One little monkey jumping on the bed
He fell off and bumped his head
Mama called the doctor and the doctor said,
"No more monkeys jumping on the bed!"

ONE, TWO, BUCKLE MY SHOE

1, 2, Buckle my shoe
3, 4, Shut the door
5, 6, Pick up sticks
7, 8, Lay them straight
9, 10, A big fat hen.
Let's get up and count again!

TEN IN THE BED

There were ten in a bed and the little one said,
"Roll over, roll over." (Make a rolling motion.)
So they all rolled over and one fell out.

There were nine in the bed and the little one said,
"Roll over, roll over."
So they all rolled over and one fell out...

(This is repeated until you get to the number one.)

There was one in the bed and the little one said,
"Good night!"

MONKEYS IN A TREE

Five little monkeys
Sitting in a tree
Teasing Mr. Crocodile: "You can't catch me."
"You can't catch me."

Along comes Mr. Crocodile
As quiet as can be
SNAP!!!
(Continue until all monkeys are gone.)
Away swims Mr. Crocodile
As full as he can be!

★ ★ ★

HUMPTY DUMPTY

Humpty Dumpty sat on a wall.
Humpty Dumpty had a great fall.
All the king's horses and all the king's men
Couldn't put Humpty together again!

★ ★ ★

TEDDY BEAR, TEDDY BEAR

Teddy Bear, Teddy Bear,
Turn around.

Teddy Bear, Teddy Bear,
Touch the ground.

Teddy Bear, Teddy Bear,
Show your shoe.

Teddy Bear, Teddy Bear,
That will do.

Teddy Bear, Teddy Bear,
Run upstairs.

Teddy Bear, Teddy Bear,
Say your prayers.

Teddy Bear, Teddy Bear,
Turn out the light.

Teddy Bear, Teddy Bear,
Say good night.

★ ★ ★

IT'S RAINING, IT'S POURING

It's raining, it's pouring,
The old man is snoring.
He went to bed
And bumped his head
And couldn't get up in the morning.

★★★

RAIN, RAIN, GO AWAY

Rain, rain, go away;
Come again another day;
Little Johnny wants to play.

★★★

JACK, BE NIMBLE

Jack, be nimble,
Jack, be quick,
Jack, jump over
The candlestick.

Jack jumped high,
Jack jumped low,
Jack jumped over
and burned his toe.

★★★

LITTLE JACK HORNER

Little Jack Horner
Sat in the corner,
Eating a Christmas pie.
He stuck in his thumb
And pulled out a plum,
And said, "What a good boy am I!"

★★★

JACK AND JILL

Jack and Jill
Went up the hill
To fetch a pail of water.
Jack fell down
And broke his crown
And Jill came tumbling after.

Up Jack got
And home did trot
As fast as he could caper.
Went to bed
To mend his head
With vinegar and brown paper.

★★★

LITTLE MISS MUFFET

Little Miss Muffet sat on a tuffet,
Eating her curds and whey.
Along came a spider,
Who sat down beside her
And frightened Miss Muffet away.

★ ★ ★

MARY HAD A LITTLE LAMB

Mary had a little lamb,
little lamb, little lamb,
Mary had a little lamb,
Its fleece was white as snow.

Everywhere that Mary went,
Mary went, Mary went,
Everywhere that Mary went,
The lamb was sure to go.

It followed her to school one day,
school one day, school one day,
It followed her to school one day,
Which was against the rules.

It made the children laugh and play,
laugh and play, laugh and play,
It made the children laugh and play,
To see a lamb at school.

So the teacher turned him out
turned him out
turned him out
So the teacher turned him out
And sent him straight away.

★ ★ ★

MARY, MARY, QUITE CONTRARY

Mary, Mary, quite contrary,
How does your garden grow?
With silver bells and cockleshells,
And pretty maids all in a row.

★★★

PETER, PETER, PUMPKIN EATER

Peter, Peter, pumpkin eater,
Had a wife and couldn't keep her;
He put her in a pumpkin shell
And there he kept her very well.

★★★

FUZZY WUZZY

Fuzzy Wuzzy
Was a bear
Fuzzy Wuzzy
Had no hair
Fuzzy Wuzzy
Wasn't fuzzy, was he?

Was he bare?

★★★

ITSY BITSY SPIDER

The Itsy Bitsy spider
Climbed up the water spout;
Down came the rain
And washed the spider out;
Out came the sun
And dried up all the rain;
So the Itsy Bitsy spider
Climbed up the spout again.

POP! GOES THE WEASEL

All around the mulberry bush
The monkey chased the weasel.
The monkey thought 'twas all in fun.
Pop! goes the weasel.

★ ★ ★

DIDDLE, DIDDLE, DUMPLING

Diddle, diddle, dumpling,
my son, John,
Went to bed
with his trousers on,
One shoe off
and one shoe on!
Diddle, diddle, dumpling,
my son, John!

LITTLE BOY BLUE

Little boy blue,
Come blow your horn!
The sheep's in the meadow;
The cow's in the corn.
Where is the boy
Who looks after the sheep?
He's under the haystack,
Fast asleep.
Will you wake him?
No, not I,
For if I do,
He's sure to cry.

★★★

STAR LIGHT, STAR BRIGHT

Star light, star bright,
First star I see tonight,
I wish I may, I wish I might,
Have the wish I wish tonight.

★★★

What Children Need to Learn to READ

Chapter 6

Music & Songs

usic is a fun way for children to be exposed to sounds and words. Music helps build listening, language, and memory skills, and it keeps kids active in the learning process. Music often includes rhyming, which is a great way to introduce new words in a more memorable format. Very often in a song, words repeat themselves. Listening to and singing songs helps children remember new words. This is because they hear them over and over again in a sing-song way. They gain confidence in knowing what comes next. This is a wonderful part of the beginning reading process.

THE WHEELS ON THE BUS

The wheels on the bus go round and round,
round and round,
round and round.
The wheels on the bus go round and round,
all through the town.

The horn on the bus goes beep, beep, beep,
beep, beep, beep,
beep, beep, beep.
The horn on the bus goes beep, beep, beep,
all through the town.

The wipers on the bus go swish, swish, swish,
swish, swish, swish,
swish, swish, swish.
The wipers on the bus go swish, swish, swish,
all through the town.

The people on the bus go up and down,
up and down,
up and down.
The people on the bus go up and down,
all through the town.

The babies on the bus go waa, waa, waa,
waa, waa, waa,
waa, waa, waa.
The babies on the bus go waa, waa, waa,
all through the town.

The mommies on the bus go sh, sh, sh,
sh, sh, sh,
sh, sh, sh.

What Children Need to Learn to READ

The mommies on the bus go sh, sh, sh,
all through the town.

The money on the bus goes clink, clink, clink,
clink, clink, clink,
clink, clink, clink.
The money on the bus goes clink, clink, clink,
all through the town.

The doors on the bus go open and shut,
open and shut,
open and shut.
The doors on the bus go open and shut,
all through the town.

The bell on the bus goes ding, ding, ding,
ding, ding, ding,
ding, ding, ding.
The bell on the bus goes ding, ding, ding,
all through the town.

The driver on the bus says move on back,
move on back,
move on back.
The driver on the bus says move on back,
all through the town.

★★★

LITTLE BUNNY FOO-FOO

(Sing)
Little Bunny Foo-Foo (Hold up two bunny ear fingers.)
hopping through the forest (Bounce your fingers up and down.)
scooping up the field mice (Scoop with your hand.)
and bopping them on the head. (Gently bang one of your fists
onto the other.)

(Say)
Down came the Good Fairy, and she said:
"Little Bunny Foo-Foo (Swing your fingers — "no-no.")
I don't wanna to see you (Swing your fingers — "no-no.")
scooping up the field mice (Scoop with your hand.)
and bopping them on the head. (Gently bang one of your fists
onto the other.)

I'll give you 3 chances,
and if you misbehave,
I'll turn you into a Goon!"

The next day…(Sing)
Little Bunny Foo-Foo
hopping through the forest
scooping up the field mice
and bopping them on the head.

(Say)
Down came the Good Fairy, and she said:
"Little Bunny Foo-Foo
I don't wanna to see you
scooping up the field mice
and bopping them on the head.
I'll give you 2 more chances,
and if you misbehave,
I'll turn you into a Goon!"

What Children Need to Learn to READ

The next day…(Sing)
Little Bunny Foo-Foo
hopping through the forest
scooping up the field mice
and bopping them on the head.

(Say)
Down came the Good Fairy, and she said:
"Little Bunny Foo-Foo
I don't wanna to see you
scooping up the field mice
and bopping them on the head.

I'll give you 1 more chance,
and if you misbehave,
I'll turn you into a Goon!"

The next day…(Sing)
Little Bunny Foo-Foo
hopping through the forest
scooping up the field mice
and bopping them on the head.

(Say)
Down came the Good Fairy, and she said:
"Little Bunny Foo-Foo
I don't wanna to see you
scooping up the field mice
and bopping them on the head.
I gave you 3 chances and you didn't behave.
Now I'm going to turn you into a Goon! Poof!"

The moral of the story is:
Hare today, Goon tomorrow!

DO YOUR EARS HANG LOW?

Do your ears hang low?
Do they wobble to and fro?
Can you tie 'em in a knot?
Can you tie 'em in a bow?
Can you throw 'em over your shoulder,
like a continental soldier?
Do your ears hang low?

★ ★ ★

DO YOUR EARS HANG HIGH?

Do your ears hang high?
Do they reach up to the sky?
Do they drip when they're wet?
Do they stand up when they're dry?
Can you signal to your neighbor
with a minimum of labor?
Do your ears hang high?

★ ★ ★

What Children Need to Learn to READ

I'M A LITTLE TEAPOT

I'm a little teapot
Short and stout
Here is my handle (Put your hand on your hip.)
Here is my spout (Put your other arm out straight.)

When I get all steamed up
Hear me shout.
"Tip me over (Lean over in the direction of the spout.)
and pour me out!"

★ ★ ★

I'VE BEEN WORKIN' ON THE RAILROAD

I've been workin' on the railroad
All the live-long day.
I've been workin' on the railroad
Just to pass the time away.
Can't you hear the whistle blowing
Rise up so early in the morn.
Don't you hear the captain shoutin',
"Dinah, blow your horn!"
Someone's in the kitchen with Dinah
Someone's in the kitchen I know
Someone's in the kitchen with Dinah
Strumming on the old banjo.
Fee, fie, fiddleio
Fee, fie, fiddleio
Fee, fie, fiddleio,
Strummin' on the old banjo.

★ ★ ★

HOKEY POKEY

You put your (right hand) in.
You put your (right hand) out.
You put your (right hand) in.
And you shake it all about.
You do the hokey pokey,
And you turn yourself around.
That's what it's all about!

(Repeat using different body parts: hand, elbow, leg, knee, foot,
and head. Alternate right and left. Then use front side, back
side, whole self, etc.)

★★★

GRAND OLD DUKE OF YORK

The grand old Duke of York
He had ten thousand men
He marched them up to the top of the hill
And he marched them down again
And when they were up they were up
And when they were down they were down
And when they were only half-way up
They were neither up nor down!

(When it says up, stand up or jump up. When it says down,
sit or squat down. When it says half-way up, only stand
part-way up.)

★★★

I'M A NUT

I'm a little acorn round (Make a circle with thumb and forefinger.)

Lying on the cold, cold ground (Wave arm across front with palm facing down.)

Somebody came and stepped on me (Stomp foot.)

That is why I'm cracked you see (Make a zig-zag motion with forefinger.)

I'm a nut (clap, clap), in a rut (clap, clap)

I'm crazy (Circle finger around ear.)

★★★

TWINKLE, TWINKLE, LITTLE STAR

Twinkle, twinkle, little star,
How I wonder what you are,
Up above the world so high,
Like a diamond in the sky.
Twinkle, twinkle, little star,
How I wonder what you are.

★★★

OLD MACDONALD

Old MacDonald had a farm
Ee i ee i o
And on his farm he had some pigs
Ee i ee i o
With an oink-oink here
And an oink-oink there
Here an oink, there an oink
Everywhere an oink-oink
Old MacDonald had a farm
Ee i ee i o

Old MacDonald had a farm
Ee i ee i o
And on his farm he had some cows
Ee i ee i o
With a moo-moo here
And a moo-moo there
Here a moo, there a moo
Everywhere a moo-moo
Old MacDonald had a farm
Ee i ee i o

Old MacDonald had a farm
Ee i ee i o
And on his farm he had some sheep
Ee i ee i o
With a baa-baa here
And a baa-baa there
Here a baa, there a baa
Everywhere a baa-baa
Old MacDonald had a farm
Ee i ee i o

Old MacDonald had a farm
Ee i ee i o
And on his farm he had some ducks
Ee i ee i o
With a quack-quack here
And a quack-quack there
Here a quack, there a quack
Everywhere a quack-quack
Old MacDonald had a farm
Ee i ee i o

(You can continue to add different animals to this song.)

★ ★ ★

MISS MARY MACK

Miss Mary Mack, Mack, Mack
All dressed in black, black, black
With silver buttons, buttons, buttons
All down her back, back, back.

She asked her mother, mother, mother
For 50 cents, cents, cents
To see the elephants, elephants, elephants
Jump over the fence, fence, fence.

They jumped so high, high, high
They reached the sky, sky, sky
And they didn't come back, back, back
'Til the fourth of July, ly, ly!

★ ★ ★

IF YOU'RE HAPPY AND YOU KNOW IT

If you're happy and you know it, clap your hands! (Clap! Clap!)
If you're happy and you know it, clap your hands! (Clap! Clap!)
If you're happy and you know it,
And you really want to show it,
If you're happy and you know it, clap your hands! (Clap! Clap!)

If you're happy and you know it, stomp your feet! (Stomp! Stomp!)
If you're happy and you know it, stomp your feet! (Stomp! Stomp!)
If you're happy and you know it,
And you really want to show it,
If you're happy and you know it, stomp your feet! (Stomp! Stomp!)

If you're happy and you know it, shout hooray! (Hoo-Ray!)
If you're happy and you know it, shout hooray! (Hoo-Ray!)
If you're happy and you know it,
And you really want to show it,
If you're happy and you know it, shout hooray! (Hoo-Ray!)

If you're happy and you know it, do all three!
    (Clap! Clap! Stomp! Stomp! Hoo-Ray!)
If you're happy and you know it, do all three!
    (Clap! Clap! Stomp! Stomp! Hoo-Ray!)
If you're happy and you know it,
And you really want to show it,
If you're happy and you know it, do all three!
    (Clap! Clap! Stomp! Stomp! Hoo-Ray!)

★ ★ ★

A SAILOR WENT TO SEA, SEA, SEA

A sailor went to sea, sea, sea
To see what he could see, see, see
But all that he could see, see, see
Was the bottom of the deep blue sea, sea, sea

★ ★ ★

THE MORE WE GET TOGETHER

The more we get together
Together, together
The more we get together
The happier we'll be.
For your friends are my friends
And my friends are your friends.
The more we get together
The happier we'll be.

★ ★ ★

What Children Need to Learn to READ

Chapter 7

Letters & Their Sounds

Research has shown that kids with reading problems tend to have the most difficulty with how letters and sounds function within language. Letters and their sounds create the foundation and backbone of the reading process. A child can learn the names of the letters, their sounds, and how these sounds go together to make words.

ALPHABET BLOCKS

What you will need:

- ✔ Alphabet blocks (blocks with letters on them)

What to do:

- ✔ You can pick up a block or point to one, and tell your child the name of the letter on the block.

- ✔ Talk about and name the colors of the blocks. You can also sort them by color.

- ✔ Make a couple of towers of blocks and talk about which tower is taller, shorter, wider, etc. (comparison words are important for math and reading comprehension).

- ✔ You can stack them together to make words, saying the letters as you go along.

- ✔ As your child picks up a block, say the name of the letter.

- ✔ You can spell out your child's name and other words that your child is familiar with, such as ball, toy, book, dog, cat, etc.

ALPHABET BOOKS

What you will need:

✔ An alphabet book

What to do:

Reading alphabet books is a fun way to learn about letters and the beginning sounds of things. As you read the book to your child, have them fill in anything they know. If they know what a letter is, have them say the name of the letter. Point to pictures on the page, and see if they can name the pictures. Talk about how each of those words starts with the same letter sound. Emphasize the beginning sound of each word, so that they can better follow the pattern. As they get more advanced, ask them if they can think of any other things that start with that letter sound. See listing of alphabet books in Appendix B.

★★★

ALPHABET PUZZLES

What you will need:

✔ An alphabet puzzle

What to do:

As you or your child takes a letter out of the puzzle, say the name of the letter and set it down. Do the same as each letter is taken out. As your child gets more advanced, you can ask him/her to find the letter "A," the letter "G," etc. You can mix up the pieces and put them into a bag, jar, or box, and have the child pick one out at a time. See if he/she can say the name of the letter and find the spot that it fits into the puzzle. You can also put letters together to make simple words and sound them out.

MAGIC LETTER SONG

What you will need:

✔ A copy of the letter song listed below and/or a copy of the free downloadable musical version of the song (available at www.LearnersLane.com)

What to do:

Listed below are the words for each letter of the alphabet that are included in the Magic Letter Song.

When you say the letter sounds, make sure that you don't put "uh" at the end of a sound. It's not "muh." It's "mmm." It's not "nuh." It's "nnn."

By singing this song often, your child will become more familiar with the letters and their sounds. Then, when your child is having trouble remembering a letter sound, you can help her by saying the part of the *Magic Letter Song* that features the sound she is struggling with. (For example, "T is for Tiger...") That will prompt her to say the beginning sound of the word three times (t, t, t).

A is for Apple – a, a, a ("a" sound).

B is for Baseball – b, b, b ("b" sound).

C is for Candy – c, c, c ("c" sound).

D is for Dragon – d, d, d ("d" sound).

E is for Elephant – e, e, e ("e" sound).

F is for Feather – f, f, f ("f" sound).

G is for Goldfish – g, g, g ("g" sound).

H is for Hippo – h, h, h ("h" sound).

I is for Igloo – i, i, i ("i" sound).

J is for Jump rope – j, j, j ("j" sound).

K is for Kitten – k, k, k ("k" sound).

L is for Lemon – l, l, l ("l" sound).

M is for Monkey – m, m, m ("m" sound).

N is for Necklace – n, n, n ("n" sound).

O is for Octopus – o, o, o ("o" sound).

P is for Pumpkin – p, p, p ("p" sound).

Q is for Quilt – q, q, q ("q" sound).

R is for Rainbow – r, r, r ("r" sound).

S is for Scissors – s, s, s ("s" sound).

T is for Tiger – t, t, t ("t" sound).

U is for Umbrella – u, u, u ("u" sound).

V is for Vacuum – v, v, v ("v" sound).

W is for Wagon – w, w, w ("w" sound).

X is for X-ray – x, x, x ("x" sound).

Y is for Yellow – y, y, y ("y" sound).

Z is for Zipper – z, z, z ("z" sound).

Visit www.LearnersLane.com for a free download of this song.

★★★

SING AND LOOK

What you will need:

    ✔ Note cards with one capital letter printed on each card.

        OR

    ✔ Free downloadable letter flashcards available at www.LearnersLane.com

What to do:

As you sing the Magic Letter Song, hold up the flashcard with the corresponding letter on it. Change flashcards with each new letter of the song. This way, your child will tie the visual and auditory parts of learning the letters and sounds together.

MAGICAL LETTER MATCHING GAME

What you will need:

✔ Note cards with one capital letter printed on each card and a drawing or clip art of something that corresponds to the beginning sound of each of the letters on separate note cards

OR

✔ Free downloadable letter and picture flashcards available at www.LearnersLane.com

What to do:

For beginners, start the game by having the letter and picture flashcards spread out face up on a table or on the floor. Mix up the cards and have your child match the letter cards with the picture cards. Give them lots of encouragement and praise as they match the cards together. As they master the game, separate the letter and picture cards and shuffle the two decks. Then place all the letter cards on one side of the table face down and the picture cards on the other side face down. Take turns picking two cards, one from each side of the table to find a match. If no match is found, then the cards are turned back to the face down position, and the next player tries turning over two cards. Encourage them to remember where the cards are as they are turned up. Have each player place their matches in front of them and count them up at the end of the game.

Then you also can play the game with all the cards mixed up and turned face down in the center of the table. This is a bit more challenging, because your child may pick two letter cards or two picture cards instead of one of each. Remember to be positive and encouraging. The goal is to have fun with letters and sounds! Go to www.LearnersLane.com for free printable flashcards that you can download.

★★★

MAGIC LETTER FLIP GAME

What you will need:

- ✔ Note cards with one capital letter printed on each card

    OR

- ✔ Free downloadable flashcards available at
    www.LearnersLane.com

What to do:

Place the flashcards face down on the floor or a table. Take turns picking up a card and saying the name of the letter and its sound. If your child is having trouble with a letter sound, remind them of the letter song to help trigger their memory. For example, if they're having trouble remembering the sound for the letter S, say, "S is for scissors…" and they should respond with the sound "s, s, s". Have fun and encourage your child to have fun with letters and their sounds! Have them keep the letters in front of them as they say them. This will help to give them a sense of accomplishment. They may even start putting letters together in front of them to try to make words. Go to www.LearnersLane.com for free printable flashcards that you can download.

MYSTERY LETTER GAME

What you will need:

    ✔ Note cards with one capital letter printed on each card

           OR

    ✔ Free downloadable flashcards available at
       www.LearnersLane.com

What to do:

Put the flashcards into a bag. Have your child pull them out one by one, and say the name of the letter and the sound it makes. If they don't know the letter or the sound, tell them what it is and have them put it back in the bag. You can even time them to see how many cards they know in a minute or give them clues to help them remember. Go to www.LearnersLane.com for free printable flashcards that you can download.

LETTERS, LETTERS, EVERYWHERE!

What you will need:

- ✔ Construction paper or poster board
- ✔ Crayons or markers
- ✔ Magazines you can cut up
- ✔ Scissors
- ✔ Glue or glue stick

What to do:

Draw large letters on construction paper or poster board. Color them and cut them out. Put them up around your child's bedroom or playroom. You can then create drawings with your child (or cut out pictures from magazines) for words that start with each letter and put them up either on or around each letter. Or, you can make a poster with all the letters drawn out on one piece of poster board. You can draw or put a cut-out picture that starts with the letter next to each letter on the poster. Place the poster somewhere your child will see it often. It's fabulous for your child to be surrounded by letters!

★ ★ ★

MAGICAL LETTER/PICTURE DICTIONARY

What you will need:

- ✔ Magazines to cut up
- ✔ Scissors
- ✔ Construction paper
- ✔ Glue or glue stick
- ✔ Paper punch and ribbon
- ✔ Crayons or markers

What to do:

Your child can make his own letter/picture dictionary. Look through some old magazines and cut out individual letters. Make a separate page for each letter. Glue a bunch of letter A's onto the A page and then look through the magazine to find pictures of things that start with the letter A. Cut them out and paste them onto the A page. You can also draw pictures of things in your Magical Letter/Picture Dictionary! Do this for each letter of the alphabet and also create a cover for the dictionary. Then make three hole punches down the left side of each of the pages so that they line up together (this can be done beforehand or after the pages are complete). Cut three pieces of ribbon and string each one through the hole punches that you made through the entire stack of pages and the cover. Now your child will have his/her very own hand-created letter/picture dictionary!

★ ★ ★

MYSTERY BAG

What you will need:

- ✔ Paper bag
- ✔ Household items (toys, clothing, etc.)

What to do:

Collect different items from around the house or yard and place them in a paper bag. Have your child reach into the bag and pull out an item, say the name of the item, and tell what letter it starts with. Then have them pull out another item and do the same until they've "solved the mystery" of everything in the bag. As they get more advanced, have them reach into the bag, feel the object, and tell you what it is, including its beginning letter sound and name, without taking it out and looking at it. You could also have them name the ending sounds of each object.

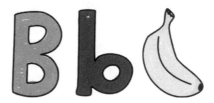

I SPY

What you will need:

✔ Just you and your child

What to do:

To play the "I Spy" game, take turns picking out something that you see around the room or outside and say, "I spy, with my little eye, something that begins with (say the letter that the item begins with)."

The other person looks around the room and lists things that they see that start with that letter until they say the one that the speaker was thinking of. Then the second player "spies" something. For example, I might see a book, so I would say, "I spy, with my little eye, something that begins with B." The other player would look around the room and list anything they see that starts with the letter B until they say "book."

Hands-On Letter Practice

MODELING MAGIC

What you will need:

✔ Play Dough or modeling clay

What to do:

Make letters and words with clay or Play Dough! You can also make creations that start with different letters of the alphabet. For example, make a mountain for the letter M.

CHALK BOARD/WHITE BOARD

What you will need:

✔ Chalk board or white board

✔ Chalk or dry erase markers

What to do:

Practice writing letters and words on a chalk board or white board. You can also draw pictures of things that start with different letters of the alphabet. For example, draw a house for the letter H.

SAND OR CORNMEAL

What you will need:

- ✔ Sand or cornmeal
- ✔ Plastic tub or 9x13 baking dish

What to do:

Put enough sand or cornmeal to cover the bottom of a tub or pan and then have your child use his/her finger to draw different letters, or pictures that start with those letters, in the sand or cornmeal. Then gently shake the pan. The letter or picture will disappear, and your child can make a new one.

SHAVING CREAM

What you will need:

- ✔ Can of shaving cream
- ✔ Kitchen table or cookie sheet

What to do:

Spray some shaving cream on a table and have your child finger-paint different letters and pictures that start with those letters. The shaving cream can be smoothed out over and over again to create new letters. This will also clean your table in the process! Just make sure your child doesn't eat the shaving cream. If you're worried about this, try whipping cream instead. (If you are worried that this activity might damage your table, put the shaving cream on a cookie sheet or other similar surface.)

FINGER PAINT

What you will need:

- ✔ Finger paint
- ✔ Finger paint paper

What to do:

Have your child finger-paint different letters and pictures that start with the letters.

ALPHABET CEREAL, COOKIES, OR CRACKERS

What you will need:

- ✔ Alphabet cereal, cookies, or crackers

What to do:

Find different letters and put them together to make words. Then eat some of them in the end! Yum! Yum!

SIDEWALK CHALK

What you will need:

- ✔ Sidewalk chalk
- ✔ Sidewalk

What to do:

You can take your letter learning to the great outdoors with sidewalk chalk. Draw letters and pictures of things that start with the different letters on the sidewalk outside your home.

What Children Need to Learn to READ

Chapter 8

Sight Words

Sight words are words that usually cannot be sounded out and that occur frequently in books, newspapers, and magazines. The Dolch Sight Word List contains 220 words that occur in 50-75% of our written language. These are also words that can't be learned by using picture clues. Once children master these words, they will know many of the words they will encounter as they read. Their reading confidence will soar, and so will their reading ability!

DOLCH SIGHT WORDS

Here are the Dolch Sight Words, in order of frequency in our written language:

GROUP 1

the	I	was	for
to	you	said	on
and	it	his	they
he	of	that	but
a	in	she	had

GROUP 2

at	look	out	we
him	is	as	am
with	her	be	then
up	there	have	little
all	some	go	down

GROUP 3

do	what	get	my
can	so	them	would
could	see	like	me
when	not	one	will
did	were	this	yes

GROUP 4

big	now	very	ride
went	long	an	into
are	no	over	just
come	came	your	blue
if	ask	its	red

GROUP 5

from	want	put	every
good	don't	too	pretty
any	how	got	jump
about	know	take	green
around	right	where	four

What Children Need to Learn to READ

GROUP 6

away	saw	ran	sleep
old	call	let	brown
by	after	help	yellow
their	well	make	five
here	think	going	six

GROUP 7

walk	again	stop	cold
two	play	off	today
or	who	never	fly
before	been	seven	myself
eat	may	eight	round

GROUP 8

tell	first	black	goes
much	try	white	write
keep	new	ten	always
give	must	does	drink
work	start	bring	once

GROUP 9

soon	has	our	warm
made	find	better	ate
run	only	hold	full
gave	us	buy	those
open	three	funny	done

GROUP 10

use	hurt	sit	under
fast	pull	which	read
say	cut	fall	why
light	kind	carry	own
pick	both	small	found

GROUP 11

wash	live	upon	thank
show	draw	these	wish
hot	clean	sing	many
because	grow	together	shall
far	best	please	laugh

MAGIC SIGHT WORD PUZZLES

What you will need:

✔ Note cards

OR

✔ Free downloadable sight word cards from www.LearnersLane.com

✔ Pen, pencil or crayon

✔ Scissors

✔ Envelopes

What to do:

Write each sight word on a note card or print the sight word cards off the above website.

Cut each card into pieces, with each piece containing one of the letters of the word. Place the word pieces into an envelope and write the word on the front of the envelope. Give your child the envelope and have them take the letters out and put the puzzle pieces together to match the written word on the front of the envelope. Then have them spell the word and say it.

★ ★ ★

SIGHT WORD MATCH

What you will need:

✔ Two sets of the same sight word cards (either downloaded from www.LearnersLane.com or copy the words from the book onto note cards. Refer to sight word lists on pages 89-92.)

What to do:

Spread out the cards and place them face down on a table. Take turns flipping up two cards at a time to see if you have a sight word match. Say each of the words. If you have a match, keep the cards in front of you. If you don't have a match, turn the cards face down again. Try to remember where the words are as you play. See how many matches you can get.

GO FISH SIGHT WORDS

What you will need:

✔ Two sets of the same sight word cards (either downloaded from www.LearnersLane.com or copy the words from the book onto note cards. Refer to sight word lists on pages 89-92.)

What to do:

Mix up the sight word cards and pass out five cards to all the players. Put the rest of the cards face down in a stack in the middle of the table. Each person will look through their cards to see if they have any sight word matches. If they do, they will read the words and place the matches in front of them. Then one person starts by asking the person to their right if they have a ___ card. They should fill in that blank with one of the sight words they're holding in their hand. If that person has the card, they must give it to the player who asked them for it. The player places the match in front of them with their other matches. If the player does not have that sight word in their hand, they tell the other person to "Go Fish," and the person has to draw a card from the stack. Then, the next player asks the player on their right if they have one of their sight word cards. Keep playing until a player has no cards in their hand. Count up the number of sight word matches that each player has. The one with the most is the winner.

What Children Need to Learn to READ

Chapter 9

Read Alouds, Listening & Comprehension

eading aloud to and with your kids is so important for helping them build their vocabulary, listening skills, and story sequencing skills.

Facts about Reading Aloud

Asking your kids questions before, during, and after reading will help build their reading comprehension skills (understanding what they are reading). Good reading comprehension comes when they can tie what they are reading to the knowledge they already possess. They will also build good vocabularies, and learn to summarize a story. They start to predict what will come next, and gain a strong understanding of the characters, the story setting, the problem that occurs in the story, and the solution or outcome that is portrayed.

WHAT'S IT ABOUT?

What you will need:

- ✔ A book that your child is reading or you are reading to them
- ✔ List of question ideas below

What to do:

Here is a list of questions you can ask your child before, during, and after reading to help them develop their reading comprehension skills. These questions can be springboards for discussions you can have about what's happening in the story. You can also discuss words that your child might not be familiar with as you read along in the story. This will help build their vocabularies and, in turn, their reading comprehension skills. You don't have to overwhelm your child each time they read. Sometimes, just ask questions here and there to see how they're processing the information they're reading.

- ✔ Looking at the title and the cover of the book, ask, "What do you think this book will be about?"
- ✔ Looking at the pictures in the book, ask, "What do you think this book will be about?"
- ✔ "What do you think will happen next?"
- ✔ "Why do you think that happened?"
- ✔ "Where does the story take place?"
- ✔ "Who are the characters in the story, and how would you describe each of them?"
- ✔ "Who is the main character, and why do you think so?"
- ✔ "Who is your favorite/least favorite character, and why?"

✔ "What would you have done in that situation?"

✔ "How could you change the ending of the story?"

✔ "What was the problem in the story, and how was it solved?"

✔ "How would you have solved the problem in the story?"

✔ "Retell the story in your own words."

✔ "How is the story similar/different to another book you have read?"

★ ★ ★

READ-A-ROUND

What you will need:

✔ A book at your child's reading level

What to do:

Take turns reading parts of the book to each other. You can stop at the end of each sentence, paragraph, page, or chapter to switch readers. Talk about what makes up a sentence (starts with a capital letter and often ends with a period). You can also talk about what makes up a paragraph (one or more sentences that usually start indented and represent a single topic or a character's spoken words).

★ ★ ★

SILLY READ-A-ROUND

What you will need:

✔ A different book for each person

What to do:

Each person picks a different book. Someone starts by reading the first sentence of their book aloud. The next person reads the first sentence of their book aloud. Keep rotating around until you come back to the first person. That person now reads the second sentence aloud. Each person in turn will read their second sentence. Then, third sentences will be read, and then fourth, and so on. This will create a very unique and entertaining story that will keep you on your toes, and should bring lots of laughs!

MOZART IN ACTION

What you will need:

✔ Children's book

✔ Paper and crayons, markers, colored pencils or paint

OR

✔ Play Dough

What to do:

As you read a story, have your child draw, paint, or sculpt with Play Dough something from the story (character, scene, etc.). When you're done reading, have your child tell you about their picture or sculpture. Through this activity, they will be working on their listening skills and comprehension, as well as their descriptive vocabularies and speaking skills. If you have a roll of butcher paper, you can roll out a four foot (approx.) strip of paper and have your child quickly sketch or watercolor-paint parts of the story as you read. Have them move across the paper as you continue reading. When you're finished reading and they're done drawing or painting, have them describe their works of art as a summary of the book or chapter you read. This will help them with story sequencing and summary skills.

BEAUTIFUL BOOKMARKS

What you will need:

- ✔ Children's book
- ✔ Construction paper or heavy duty paper
- ✔ Crayons, markers, or colored pencils

What to do:

Your child can make a different bookmark for each book they read. Take a piece of paper and cut out a thin rectangular shape. Have your child write the title of the book and the name of the author on one side of the paper. On the other side, have them draw a picture of a character from the story, or something that happened in the story. You can even have your child make one of these bookmarks to give as a gift, with a book, to a friend or family member.

GRACIOUS GRANDMA/GRANDPA

What grandma/grandpa will need:

✔ Video camera

✔ Book they would like to read to grandchild and send to them

✔ Some sort of special item or activity that follows the theme of the story to send (optional)

What to do:

Today, many of us live far away from our extended families. Here's one fun way to keep the family bond alive and help instill a love of reading in your child.

Grandma or Grandpa, or another relative or friend, can video themselves reading a special story to their special child. They can show themselves in the video and say the title and author of the book. As they read, they can show the pages of the book. They can use expression when they read and try to create different voices for the characters, if possible. Then they can send the video-recording to your child, with a copy of the book. They can also send something special that relates to the story. For example, let's say it's *When the Doorbell Rang,* by Pat Hutchins. This story has a grandma baking cookies to give to her grandchildren and their friends. So special cookies could be sent along with the recording and book. If you read *It's the Bear!,* by Jez Alborough, a small bear stuffed animal could be sent along. Have fun with this! Children will love watching these stories over and over again. The bond of love will grow stronger, as will their love of reading!

★ ★ ★

What Children Need to Learn to READ

AUDIO BOOKS AND SING-ALONGS

What you will need:

- ✔ Audio books (books on tape or CD)
- ✔ Audio cassettes or CDs with children's songs

What to do:

There are many wonderful books that have been put into audio form. Check with your local library or book store to find some that you might like. There are also enjoyable children's sing-along tapes and CDs to keep them entertained and help them to develop their listening and academic skills.

★ ★ ★

What Children Need to Learn to READ

Chapter 10

Phonics

Kids need to learn that words are made up of segments of sound. They must learn what those sounds are, and which letters or groups of letters make up each sound. Then they can learn to put them together to sound out and read words. Rhyming and being able to recognize that two words end with the same sound is a very important phonetic pre-reading skill. In addition to the following phonics activities, please also refer to Chapters 5 and 6 for more fun ways to build on your child's rhyming skills.

"Research has shown conclusively that children's phonemic awareness, their understanding that spoken words can be divided into separate sounds, is one of the best predictors of their success in learning to read."

Texas Education Agency

WACKY WORDS

What you will need:

- ✔ Paper
- ✔ Scissors
- ✔ Pencil, pen, or crayon
- ✔ 3 small tubs (yogurt or butter tubs)

What to do:

Cut a sheet of paper into small squares of paper, about 1" x 1" or so. On each piece of paper, write a letter of the alphabet. Make two slips of paper for each consonant (see below), and one for each vowel. Then put one set of consonants in an empty yogurt tub (or margarine container, etc.) and put the other set of consonants in another tub. Place the slips of paper with vowels on them in yet another tub. Place the tubs in front of your child in this order: tub of consonants, then a tub of vowels, and then a tub of consonants. Have your child pick a slip from each tub and place them in that same order. Have them sound out the three-letter word that they created (it might be a real word or a silly word). Ask them if it's a word they're familiar with or a silly word. Have them put the letters back in the tubs and mix them up. Have them pick three new slips of paper and repeat the process.

Consonants: B,C,D,F,G,H,J,K,L,M,N,P,Q,R,S,T,V,W,X,Y,Z

Vowels: A,E,I,O,U

WORD FAMILIES

What you will need:

✔ Paper and pencil

What to do:

You can play around with word families. Take out the first letter of a word and replace it with another letter to make a new word that rhymes with the original word. See how many different words you can make for each one you choose. Here are some examples:

WORD FAMILIES

DOG   __OG – (LOG, FOG, BOG, etc.)

CAT   __AT – (BAT, RAT, SAT, etc.)

RUG   __UG – (BUG, DUG, LUG, etc.)

DAD   __AD – (FAD, SAD, MAD, etc.)

HOT   __OT – (NOT, TOT, LOT, etc.)

BAG   __AG – (RAG, SAG, LAG, etc.)

FUN   __UN – (RUN, SUN, BUN, etc.)

LIGHT   __IGHT – (SIGHT, NIGHT, RIGHT, etc.)

You can also say three words (two that rhyme and one that doesn't). Have your child tell you which one doesn't fit the pattern. For example:

boy, toy, **box**

tag, **fun**, rag

log, lip, sip

FILL IN THE BLANK

What you will need:

- ✔ Nursery rhymes from Chapter 5

  OR

- ✔ Mother Goose book

What to do:

Pick your favorite nursery rhyme, and as you say the rhyme, leave out a part for your child to say. Have fun going back and forth with each other. Your child can start a rhyme and let you fill in the blanks.

★★★

SEE AND SOUND

What you will need:

- ✔ No supplies needed

What to do:

Point things out as you're driving, like another car, and ask what sound it starts with or what letter it starts with. Say: "I see a car! What sound does car start with?" or "I see a car! What letter does car start with?" You can also try middle and ending sounds. As your child gets more advanced, you can do this game by asking them to spell the words. You can switch it around to have your child ask you to sound or spell things that they find.

★★★

What Children Need to Learn to READ

RHYME TIME

What you will need:

- ✔ Magazine to cut up
- ✔ Scissors
- ✔ Paper
- ✔ Glue, glue stick, or tape
- ✔ Stapler, or paper punch and ribbon

What to do:

Cut out pictures with your child from a magazine that go with good rhyming words like dog and cat. Create a cover, and then glue, tape, or staple each picture on a separate piece of paper. Staple or paper punch and lace the pages together to make a book. Turn to each page and come up with as many words that rhyme with the picture word as you both can think of. Write them all on the page with the picture. For example, if you have a picture of a cat, you can write bat, sat, mat, fat, rat, hat, pat, etc. Your child will have fun going back and reading their own rhyming book.

★ ★ ★

PICTURE WORD CARDS

What you will need:

✔ 3x5 note cards with a picture illustrating a simple word, either drawn or printed off a clip-art program. Under the picture, write the word, and leave an underlined space for a missing letter. (Start with the first letter missing, then the last letter missing, then the middle letter missing.)

OR

✔ Free downloadable picture word cards from www.LearnersLane.com

✔ OPTIONAL: Small box or bag from which to draw the cards out randomly

What to do:

These cards can help children learn the beginning, middle, or ending letters/sounds of words. Each card will have a picture illustrating a word, and under the picture will be the written word, with the beginning, middle, or end letter missing. After you have the word cards, you can mix them up and place them face down, or draw them randomly out of a box or bag. Take turns picking a card and filling in the missing letter or sound as you say the word. You can also spell the word. You can make your own picture cards using Classroom Clipart, or Microsoft Clip Gallery, or you can download them from www.LearnersLane.com.

Picture Cards:

(picture of word – example: cat)

_at

ca_

c_t

MYSTERY SOUNDS

What you will need:

✔ No supplies needed

What to do:

Ask your child, "Can you guess the word I'm sounding out?" Then pick a word and say the sounds slowly. See if they can put the sounds together to make the word. Then switch and have your child sound out a word for you to guess.

"/b/ /i/ /g/" big

SYLLABLES

What you will need:

✔ No supplies needed

What to do:

Practicing counting out the syllables of words with your child will help them see that different groups of sounds are put together to make words. Clap out syllables with your child. To make it more fun for them, try using their name. For example: Kevin (clap out "Ke" "vin" – 2 syllables), Brittany (clap out "Brit" "tan" "y" – 3 syllables). Then try other words (ball – "ball" – only 1 syllable) (kitten – "kit" "ten" – 2 syllables), etc.

CLAP! STOMP! JUMP! — SILLY SOUNDS

What you will need:

✔ No supplies needed

What to do:

Choose some simple words to sound out for or with your child. As you sound them out, clap your hands once for each sound. Then try stomping your feet or jumping with each sound. You can try this with many different body movements. Here is a list of some movements that you can try, but I'm sure that you can think of many more. Movement helps students focus on the letter sounds and makes it much more memorable and fun!

/b/ /u/ /s/

Clap your hands

Stomp your feet

Jump up and down

Touch your toes

Pat your head

Snap your fingers

Chapter 11

Writing

Reading and writing go hand in hand. Reading helps develop writing skills, and writing helps develop reading skills. Talk with your kids about what they're writing. Don't worry much about misspellings (invented spelling). As they read and write more, their spelling will improve over time. Encourage them to have fun with their writing, and to write often.

DICTATED STORIES

What you will need:

- ✔ Paper
- ✔ Pencil or pen
- ✔ Crayons, markers, or colored pencils
- ✔ Stapler, or paper punch and ribbon

What to do:

If your child can't write yet, have him/her dictate a story or experience to you. Write it down. Your child can illustrate it, or have them draw a picture first and describe it to you as you write their words on the page. Create a cover, and then staple (or paper punch and lace) the pages together to make a book. You and your child will enjoy reading their story over and over again!

REPETITIVE RHYMING STORYBOOK

What you will need:

- ✔ Paper
- ✔ Pencil or pen
- ✔ Crayons, markers, or colored pencils
- ✔ Stapler, or paper punch and ribbon

What to do:

Take a repetitive rhyme or story, like:

Little green frog

Sits on a log,

Little green frog

Sees a from the log

Write this down on numerous pieces of paper, or write it down and make copies, and have your child fill in the blanks with different things you want the frog to see. Then have them draw pictures of the different things that the frog sees. Create a cover. Next, staple (or paper punch and lace) the pages together and your child will have his very own hand-made book.

★★★

NAME POEMS

What you will need:

- ✔ Paper
- ✔ Pencil or pen
- ✔ Crayons, markers, or colored pencils

What to do:

Write down your child's name in a vertical column. Then you and your child pick words or phrases that start with each letter of his/her name that tell something about your child. Write the words and phrases next to the letters of his/her name to create a poem. Your child can illustrate the poem by drawing a picture of themselves, or of some of the things mentioned in the poem.

BRIANA

Briana is creative

Reads a lot

Is happy when drawing

Always loves to play with friends

Nuzzles kittens

Always loves to write and act

★ ★ ★

PICTURE POWER

What you will need:

- ✔ Paper
- ✔ Pencil or pen
- ✔ Crayons, markers, or colored pencils
- ✔ OPTIONAL: Scissors, tape, or glue stick, and clip art or magazines to cut pictures from

What to do:

Write a short story or pick out a story you already know. Replace certain words in the story with drawings, clip art or magazine cut-outs. For example, whenever you see the word "house", take out the word and replace it with a picture of a house. Do this for different words in a story. You can replace the word, "tree", with a picture of the tree. Place a picture of a balloon wherever you see the word "balloon". Then have fun reading the story using the words and pictures. This is called a rebus story.

RAVING REPORTER

What you will need:

- ✔ Paper
- ✔ Pencil or pen
- ✔ Stapler, or paper punch and ribbon
- ✔ OPTIONAL: Camera

What to do:

Have your child identify people who he/she would like to interview (friend, neighbor, grandparent, teacher, etc.), and create a list of questions to ask them. The goal is to learn as much about their interview subjects as possible. During the interview, your child will write down their answers or have their subjects write them down. Compile all the interviews to make a *People I Know* journal or book. Create a cover with this title, and then staple (or paper punch and lace) the pages together. You might want to take a picture of each person interviewed and put it next to their answers in the book. You and your child will have fun reading through it to see what was learned about your family and friends. Here are some possible questions to ask:

- ✔ What is your full name?
- ✔ When were you born?
- ✔ Where were you born?
- ✔ What different places have you lived?
- ✔ What is your favorite color?
- ✔ What is your favorite food?
- ✔ What is your favorite game?
- ✔ What is your favorite book?

What Children Need to Learn to READ

- ✔ What was your favorite thing to do when you were a kid, and what do you like to do now?

- ✔ What is the funniest thing that ever happened to you?

- ✔ What is the most embarrassing thing that ever happened to you?

- ✔ What was the scariest thing that ever happened to you?

- ✔ What do/did you want to be when you grew up?

- ✔ What is/was your favorite subject in school?

★ ★ ★

SILLY STORY

What you will need:

- ✔ Paper

- ✔ Pencil or pen

What to do:

Create a silly story with your family or friends. Have your child write or dictate a sentence to you as the opening for a story. "Once upon a time there was…" (Have them continue the sentence). Then pass the paper to the next person, who will write the next sentence. Keep passing the paper and writing sentences until you feel you have come to the end of your story. Conclude with "The End." Go back and read the story aloud and see how funny it came out! You can also do this verbally (without writing it down). This will be quicker, and you can keep the story moving along. However, you will not have a hard copy to read over again for additional entertainment!

★ ★ ★

READING BEAR

What you will need:

- ✔ Spiral-bound notebook
- ✔ Teddy bear
- ✔ Pencils or pen
- ✔ Crayons, markers or colored pencils
- ✔ OPTIONAL: Camera

What to do:

This is a great idea for a classroom or a group of friends or neighbors, or even a child on his/her own. Pick out a stuffed animal (it could be a teddy bear or any other animal the group likes). Get a spiral-bound notebook. Have the kids take turns taking Reading Bear home with them for a couple of days. Your child should bring the bear with them on all of their outings, and while they are doing things at home. Your child can take pictures of the bear as they go about their day. At the end of each day, have your child make journal entries about what Reading Bear did with them today. Your child can mount the pictures, or draw pictures to go with their writing about Reading Bear's adventures. Then pass the journal and the bear on to the next child. The children can look at the pictures and read about what Reading Bear has experienced with each child. They will be excited to see what the other kids have done, and will cherish their special time with Reading Bear!

★★★

PHOTO-JOURNALIST

What you will need:

- ✔ Construction paper
- ✔ Pencil or pen
- ✔ Tape or glue
- ✔ Stapler, or paper punch and ribbon
- ✔ Camera

What to do:

Take pictures as you and your child take a walk, go on an outing, or just do something around the house. Your child would love to take the pictures if you feel comfortable with that. Print out the pictures or get them developed. Have your child place the pictures on construction paper in the order the events of the day took place. Glue or tape them down to construction paper or another firm type of scrap book paper to make a book. Have your child write or dictate to you what happened at the time each picture was taken. Create a cover, then staple (or paper punch and lace) the pages together. Your child will have created his/her own special book. He/she can read and look at the pictures, remembering the experiences, while developing their reading, vocabulary, and sequencing skills.

JIVIN' JOURNAL/TRIP JOURNAL

What you will need:

- ✔ Spiral-bound notebook, journal, or sheets of lined paper
- ✔ Pencil or pen
- ✔ Stapler, or paper punch and ribbon
- ✔ OPTIONAL: Crayons, markers, colored pencils, camera

What to do:

Purchase a journal or spiral-bound notebook, or staple (or paper punch and lace) a bunch of lined paper together. At the end of each day, have your child write or dictate their experiences in their very own journal. Periodically, go back and read with them what had previously been written. They will love to see the story of their own life unfold. They will begin to see how many experiences and adventures that they've had. You can also have them write about their feelings. Prompt them with questions like "How did you feel when…?"

"What was your favorite part of today, and why?"

"What was the hardest thing you did today, and why?"

"What is something new you learned today?"

"What is something new you'd like to do or learn tomorrow?"

Your child can illustrate their journal. Remember to put the date at the top of each entry. When you go on vacation, your child can create a Trip Journal. At the end of each day, they can write about what they saw and did, and illustrate it. Photos that you take on your travels can be included. It's fun to put in other mementos, like maps, postcards, ticket stubs, pressed flowers, etc. — anything to remind your child of the adventure they had!

★ ★ ★

JOURNAL SWAP

What you will need:

- ✔ Spiral-bound notebook, or sheets of lined paper
- ✔ Pencil or pen
- ✔ Stapler, or paper punch and ribbon

What to do:

You will need a spiral-bound notebook or a bunch of papers stapled (or tied) together to make a journal. Have your child choose a friend, neighbor, or family member they would like to correspond with. Check with that person to see if they're willing to write letters back and forth. Have your child start by jotting down a letter to that person on the first page of the journal. Make sure that they put the date at the top. Have them write about what they've been doing, what things they like, etc., and have them ask questions of the person they're corresponding with. Then give the journal to the other person and have them respond on the next page by answering the questions, talking about themselves, and asking questions of your child. Keep trading back and forth, and continue the correspondence as long as they both wish to do so. They will get to know each other better, and your child will build their reading and writing skills in the process.

★ ★ ★

"YOU'VE GOT MAIL!"

What you will need:

- ✔ Paper
- ✔ Pencil or pen
- ✔ Envelope
- ✔ Stamp

What to do:

Kids love to get mail! Have your child write or dictate letters to family, friends, and the authors or illustrators of their favorite books, etc., and send the letters off in the mail. Have them write questions as well as writing about what they've been doing lately. If they write to an author, they can explain why they liked their book, and ask questions about how they got started writing, how they get their ideas, etc. Your child will love to go with you to check the mailbox in hopes of receiving a special letter. You can also help them send emails, and watch them get excited to see new email messages come into the "in box" for them!

★★★

THE JOKE'S ON YOU!
CREATE YOUR OWN JOKE BOOK!

What you will need:

- ✔ Joke book
- ✔ Spiral-bound notebook or sheets of paper
- ✔ Pencil or pen
- ✔ Stapler, or paper punch and ribbon
- ✔ Crayons, markers, or colored pencils

What to do:

Read joke books with your child. You and your child can practice telling jokes, and try them out on others. See Appendix B for a list of some wonderful children's joke books. Your child can make their very own joke book. Have them pick their favorite jokes and ask others to tell them their favorite jokes. Compile them in a notebook, or put them down on papers and staple (or tie) the pages together with a cover page on top. Your child can illustrate the book.

★ ★ ★

What Children Need to Learn to READ

Chapter 12

Word Play

Having fun with words and language helps children get excited about reading, and also helps them build their reading skills. The more kids are exposed to words and word play activities, the more skills they learn, and the more successful they will be in reading.

MAGIC WORD LABELS

What you will need:

✔ Post-it notes

✔ Marker

OR

✔ Downloadable word cards from www.LearnersLane.com

What to do:

Turn your house into a reading lab for your child! You can write your own household words on Post-it notes, or go to www.LearnersLane.com for free downloadable word cards and put them up around your house. For example, place the word "window" on a window, the word "door" on a door, the word "wall" on the wall, the word "cupboard" on a cupboard. Put up as many word cards as you can, and point them out often. Imagine how far ahead in reading your child will be when he/she sees common words around the house, over and over again. In no time at all, he/she will be reading those words on his/her own! And how fun it is to see the excitement in their eyes when they begin to read and start down the road to reading success!

IN OTHER WORDS!

What you will need:

- ✔ Paper
- ✔ Pencil

What to do:

Choose a word or phrase and see how many other words you can make from the letters in those words. For example, if you choose the word "vacation," some of the words you can make include:

VACATION

cat	it
at	action
not	no
on	can
in	van

Try these words as well for some summertime fun, or pick your own words. The sky's the limit!

Sunshine

Sand castle

Barbecue

Swimming

★ ★ ★

ORDER! ORDER! ALPHABETICAL ORDER!

What you will need:

- ✔ Paper
- ✔ Pencil OR
- ✔ Old magazine
- ✔ Scissors OR
- ✔ 3x5 note cards

                OR

- ✔ Free downloadable letter cards from www.LearnersLane.com

What to do:

Take a walk outside with your child and have them write down the things they see. When you get home, see if they can put the words in alphabetical order. You can also do this by cutting out words from a magazine or newspaper and having your child lay them out and rearrange them into alphabetical order.

For younger kids, you can work with the alphabet letters themselves. Write down each letter of the alphabet on separate 3x5 note cards, or download the letter cards from our website at www.LearnersLane.com, or you can use magnetic fridge letters, etc. Mix up the letters, and have your child put them into alphabetical order. It might help to sing the ABC song as you go, to help them remember what comes next.

SECRET CODES

What you will need:

- ✔ Paper
- ✔ Pencil

What to do:

Creating secret codes to crack is a great way to bust out of any slump of boredom! How great to be able to work on math and reading skills at the same time. A simple code is to replace each letter of the alphabet with a number (A=1, B=2, C=3 and so on). Then you can have your child write words and sentences in the number code and give them to someone else to decode. They can give the other person the key to crack the code, or have them try to figure out the pattern and crack the code on their own. For example, the words "Reading is Fun" would translate to (18,5,1,4,9,14,7/9,19/6,21,14).

★ ★ ★

CAN YOU SPY WHAT I SPY?

What you will need:

- ✔ Just you and your child

What to do:

Prompt your child by asking them, "Can you spy something _____?" Fill in with words such as (yellow, blue, tall, short, round, pointed, fast, slow, etc.). When they find something that matches, you can ask them to spy something else. They can also ask you to spy something.

★ ★ ★

CREATIVE COOKS

What you will need:

- ✔ Cookbook
- ✔ Recipe ingredients
- ✔ Measuring utensils

What to do:

Cooking together with your children is lots of fun! Cooking helps kids with reading skills, math skills, and following directions, and it is a great way to bond with your children. Children can learn an important life skill, and they will feel proud for being able to make a meal or a dessert for everyone to share! Yum! Yum!

There are many children's cookbooks with simple and delicious recipes to follow. There is a list in Appendix B at the end of this book.

SCAVENGER HUNT

What you will need:

- ✔ Paper
- ✔ Pencil
- ✔ OPTIONAL: Bag to put items in as they are found

What to do:

Make a list of things that your child might find around the house or in the yard. Have them go around with the list, search for everything on the list, and mark them off as they find them. You can have them collect the items as they go, or just check them off. Here are a couple of ideas for your lists.

AROUND THE HOUSE	OUTSIDE
❏ Sock	❏ Leaf
❏ Cracker	❏ Rock
❏ Book	❏ Pine cone
❏ Pillow	❏ Twig
❏ Stuffed animal	❏ Insect
❏ Plastic cup	❏ Weed

★ ★ ★

COOL CARDS

What you will need:

- ✔ Old greeting cards
- ✔ Scissors
- ✔ Glue stick
- ✔ Construction paper
- ✔ Pencil, crayons, markers, or colored pencils
- ✔ OPTIONAL: Stickers

What to do:

Save greeting cards that you and your children have received or have others save their old cards for you. Then have your child cut out pictures from the cards and glue them onto a folded piece of construction paper to make their own card. Then have them write or dictate what they would like to say for the special occasion. They can embellish their card with their own drawings, or add stickers to it. What a creative way to recycle!

★ ★ ★

WORD HUNT

What you will need:

- ✔ 3x5 note cards
- ✔ Pencil, or
- ✔ Downloadable sight word or letter cards from www.LearnersLane.com

What to do:

Write words that can be easily sounded out onto note cards. Hide them around the house or yard, and have your child hunt for the words. When they find a word, have them sound it out and then look for another word. See how many words they can find. You can do this with the sight words from Chapter 8, too. Many of these words need to be memorized, because they cannot be sounded out. For younger children, you can do a letter hunt. Write down a letter on each note card, and hide them for your child to find, say, and sound.

★★★

HOLLYWOOD HERE WE COME!
OUR HOME MOVIES!

What you will need:

✔ One of your home movies

What to do:

Sit down and watch home movies or videos of your child and family. Reminisce about what happened at the time, what the emotions were, what happened before and after, and talk about the sequence of events. Ask them who was in the movie, and ask them to summarize or re-tell what happened. Your child will love seeing themselves on the screen, and he/she will also be developing excellent memory and pre-reading skills.

Chapter 13

Games! Games! Games!

There are some amazing commercial games that can be played for fun and learning! The following is a list of games that are great fun to play and help develop reading skills. Please visit www.LearnersLane.com to learn where to find many of these games and other excellent learning games.

- ✔ Alphabet Activity Mats – by Lakeshore
- ✔ Alphabet Quizmo – by World Class Learning Materials
- ✔ Alphabet Squiggle Game – by University Games
- ✔ Baffle Gab – by Baffle Gab, LLC
- ✔ Initial Consonants Bingo, Ages 4 and Up – by Trend Enterprises Inc.
- ✔ Boggle Junior – by Hasbro
- ✔ The Cat in the Hat Board Game – by University Games
- ✔ Cause and Effect – by World Class Learning Materials
- ✔ Context Clues – by World Class Learning Materials
- ✔ Creepy Cave Consonant Matching Game – by Learning Resources
- ✔ Dr. Seuss ABC Board Game – by University Games

- ✔ Hooked on Phonics – by Hooked on Phonics
- ✔ Leapfrog Letter Factory Board Game – by Leapfrog
- ✔ Learning Resources Pharaoh's Phonics Game – by Learning Resources
- ✔ Letter Detective – by Ravensburger
- ✔ Pirate Island, A Reading for Details Game – by Lakeshore
- ✔ The Phonics Game – by Myrna Culbreath and Sandra Marshak
- ✔ Python Path Word-Ending Game – by Learning Resources
- ✔ Read and Rhyme by Lakeshore
    - – Short Vowels
    - – Long Vowels
- ✔ Rhyming Sounds Game – by Smethport Specialty Company
- ✔ Scrabble Junior - by Hasbro
- ✔ Scrabble Junior Disney Edition – by Hasbro
- ✔ Sequence for Kids – by Jax Ltd. Inc.
- ✔ Smart Mouth – by Thinkfun
- ✔ Sound-It-Out Puzzles – by Lakeshore
    - – Vowel Combinations
    - – Blends
    - – Digraphs
- ✔ Soundtooning – by Kaplan Early Learning Company
- ✔ Story Wands – by Lakeshore
- ✔ Sunken Treasure Adventure Phonics Beginning Blends Game – by Learning Resources
- ✔ Using Context Clues Riddle of the Ruins – by Lakeshore
- ✔ WordXchange Junior – by Prodijeux Inc.

★ ★ ★

Chapter 14

Book Parties

For Birthdays or Just Because

We're always looking for fun party ideas for our kids. We get tired of the same old things, year after year. Why not have a great party and a great learning experience at the same time? A fun-filled book party is just the answer.

INVITATIONS

What you will need:

- ✔ Paper
- ✔ Crayons, markers, or colored pencils
- ✔ OPTIONAL: Books to send along with the invitations

What to do:

Have your child help you create and send invitations to his/her friends. The invitation could be shaped like a book, or could be a book itself, with a note attached. If you send a book with each invitation, have your child help pick out one of his/her current favorite books, or a book that he/she would like to read. Send the invitation or book to each guest, and have them read it ahead of time, to get them excited about the party.

★★★

DRESS-UP

What you will need:

- ✔ No materials needed. Kids can come dressed up in costumes.

  OR

- ✔ Have some dress-up clothes available for guests to put on when they arrive.

What to do:

Have the party guests dress up as a character from a book, or as any of their favorite story characters.

BOOK BUDDIES

What you will need:

- ✔ No materials needed. Each child can bring a favorite stuffed animal.

  OR

- ✔ Provide a small, inexpensive stuffed animal or plastic animal for each child to keep.

What to do:

Have guests bring a favorite doll or stuffed animal to the book party as their reading buddy, or pass out little plastic or stuffed bears, etc., to the guests, as their reading buddy for the party, and to take with them to read with at home.

READ TO KIDS

What you will need:

- ✔ Children's book – See appendices at the end of the book for great children's book suggestions.

What to do:

Sit down with the kids and their reading buddies and read the book the party is celebrating.

DRAW OR PAINT

What you will need:

- ✔ Paper
- ✔ Crayons, markers, or colored pencils

What to do:

Have the kids draw a picture of something from the story, share their pictures with the group, and describe what's happening in the picture.

★ ★ ★

What Children Need to Learn to READ

ACT IT OUT

What you will need:

- ✔ Children's book – See appendices at the end of the book for great children's book suggestions.

What to do:

Place the children into groups, and have each group act out a part of the story for the rest of the party-goers.

BOOK BAGS

What you will need:

- ✔ Plain canvas book bags

- ✔ Permanent markers

- ✔ OPTIONAL: Glitter glue, foam stick-on shapes, sequins, iron-on designs, etc.

What to do:

Purchase book bags ahead of time and have the kids decorate them with glitter glue, foam stick-on shapes or letters, and/or sequins or iron-on designs (adults only—using the iron). They can also write their names on the bags with permanent markers.

BOOKMARKS

What you will need:

- ✔ Rectangular strips of construction paper
- ✔ Crayons, markers, or colored pencils
- ✔ OPTIONAL: Clear contact paper to laminate the bookmarks

What to do:

Pre-cut strips of construction paper into rectangular book-marks. Have the kids decorate them with crayons and markers. You can even laminate them with clear contact paper after the kids are done coloring them to make them sturdier.

CAKE AND TREATS

What you will need:

- ✔ Cake mix
- ✔ Frosting
- ✔ OPTIONAL: Gummy worms (Book worms)

What to do:

Make a cake shaped like a book, and write the title of the book on the top with decorator frosting. (See Appendix B for websites on kids' party cake ideas.) You can also make a cake shaped like a letter of the alphabet (the first letter of your child's name would be a great one to choose for a birthday party). You could put gummy worms ("book worms") on the top, or pass them out as an extra treat.

BOOK WALK

What you will need:

- ✔ Different children's books for kids to pick from and take home
- ✔ Paper (at least as many pieces of paper as kids at the party)
- ✔ Marker
- ✔ Cup
- ✔ Music

What to do:

This game is played just like the traditional cakewalk game. However, instead of picking out a cake at the end, they will each get to pick out a book to take home. Draw different letters of the alphabet on separate pieces of paper. Make sure you have at least as many letter papers as children at the party. Place the letter papers around the room in a circle. Then write each letter on a small piece of paper and place them all in a cup. Have the children stand by a letter paper to start. Turn on some music and have them walk around the circle. When the music stops, have them stop by a letter. Pick out a letter from the cup and the person standing by that letter can go pick out a book to take home. Continue playing until each child has picked out a book. You can provide a variety of books for them to choose from, or you can ask each guest to bring a new or used book with them for the book walk game. This way, each child will leave with a special book that they can read at home — with their reading bear buddy, of course!

★ ★ ★

Chapter 15

Beginning Readers Book Clubs

A **great way to get kids to have fun** with books and practice reading skills is to set up a children's book club. You can set it up any way you wish. You could have kids read the same book at home, and get together as a group to talk about the characters, favorite parts of the story, parts that surprised them, etc. Each child might come with a few questions to ask the others. You could mix up the questions, and then draw them randomly to discuss. The children can also act out parts of the story.

You might also set up the club to work on basic reading skills. For the pre-readers, play letter and sound games, and read a book to them and discuss it. For beginning readers, play with the sight word puzzle cards, play phonics-based games, and read a chapter of a book each time you meet. At the conclusion of the story, have a book party based on the book. You could also have a Book-of-the-Month Club. The students would read the same book at home and then come for an event like a dessert night to do an activity based on the book, discuss the book, and have treats. You can rotate the meetings at the children's houses each month.

"Look What I Read!" Reading Goals Sheets

Reading a bit each day keeps kids involved and intrigued. What better way to encourage reading than with the "Look What I Read!" Reading Goals Sheets?

Have your child or each child in the reading group make a weekly reading goal for themselves, and track that goal by writing down all the books or chapters of books that they read or have read to them. If they read a chapter book, they can count each chapter as a book on their reading chart. See the Reading Goals Sheet on page 194-195 or download it from www.LearnersLane.com.

If you're working with a book club reading group, have them take their Reading Goals Sheets home with them to keep track of books they read and books that are read to them. Have them bring the sheet each time you meet. You can check it off, and set a new reading goal. You could also give them each a reward for completing this activity. A small sticker or stamp is a great incentive for a child. Create a chart for each student to put their stickers or stamps on. See page 196 or use the one from www.LearnersLane.com.

If they bring back their Reading Goals Sheets, they get a sticker or stamp, and they also get a sticker or stamp if they reached their reading goal. In addition, you can give them a sticker or stamp each time they come to the book club. They can earn up to a total of 3 stickers or stamps each time. Once they fill up the spaces on the sticker/stamp chart, you could offer them a small reading prize, if you wish. On the first day of the reading group, you can show them the prize that they will get if they fill up their whole reading chart. After some length of time (3 months, 6 months, a year, etc.), you can compile each child's Reading Goals Sheets together into a "Look What I Read!" book. Each child will love to see and remember all the books they've read or have had read to them. They will be surprised by what avid readers they have become!

Reading Certificate

After your child completes their Reading Goals Sheet, award them with a reading certificate to recognize their reading efforts.

See page 197 or go to www.LearnersLane.com for a free downloadable reading certificate.

What Children Need to Learn to READ

Chapter 16

Tongue Twisters

tongue twister is a funny sentence or phrase that is challenging to say. A tongue twister should be repeated as quickly as possible to get the full effect. It is entertaining to hear yourself or someone else stumble on the words and sounds. Saying tongue twisters is not only entertaining, however. Tongue twisters help kids to hear and recognize patterns of sounds. Many tongue twisters repeat the same beginning sound over and over again. Tongue twisters can also help kids develop verbal agility skills. Some tongue twisters help kids to learn to quickly move their mouths back and forth from forming a single sound to a blended sound, which is very hard to do. Speech therapists use tongue twisters to help develop students' speaking skills and fluency.

Try the following examples with your child:

- ✔ Six slippery snails slid slowly seaward.
- ✔ How much wood could a wood chuck chuck, if a wood chuck could chuck wood?
- ✔ I scream, you scream, we all scream for ice cream!
- ✔ She sells sea shells by the sea shore.

✔ Fuzzy Wuzzy was a bear, Fuzzy Wuzzy had no hair, Fuzzy Wuzzy wasn't fuzzy... was he???

✔ Peter Piper picked a peck of pickled peppers.
If Peter Piper picked a peck of pickled peppers,
where's the peck of pickled peppers Peter Piper picked?

✔ Rubber baby-buggy bumpers

✔ Silly Sally slid down a slippery slide.

✔ Six sick snakes sit by the sea.

✔ Toy boat, toy boat, toy boat.

Author's Note

Children who get behind in reading suffer in many ways. Self-esteem and learning in all other subject areas can begin to wane. In contrast, children who start "learning to read" early will then be "reading to learn." After they master the basics of reading, they will be able to move ahead much more quickly in all other subject areas.

If we pledge to start using these simple reading strategies with our children from a very early age, we can combat illiteracy and help every child achieve their true potential through reading.

★★★

We would love to hear from you! Please send us an email at info@LearnersLane.com and give us your feedback. Tell us what you liked best, what you would like to see in future books or editions, and any ideas you have for games or activities that we might include in our next edition. We would also love to hear your personal success stories related to the ideas, suggestions, games or activities discussed in *What Children Need to Learn to READ*. You can also send your feedback, ideas, and stories to us by mail at: Learners Lane, P.O. Box 2303, Redmond, WA 98073.

What Children Need to Learn to READ

Resources: Helping Your Child Become a Reader

From the
U.S. Department of Education
Office of Communications and Outreach
Helping Your Child Become a Reader
Washington, D.C., 2005

CHILDREN'S BOOKS

Babies

Brown, Margaret Wise. *Goodnight Moon*. Harper Collins, 1997. A little rabbit says goodnight to all the things in his room and, finally, to the Moon.

Johnson, Angela. *Mama Bird, Baby Birds*. Orchard, 1994. Joshua and his sister, two young African-American children, watch a mother bird feeding its babies.

Wells, Rosemary. *Max's Bedtime*. Dial, 1998. Even though Max's sister offers him her stuffed animals, he cannot sleep without his red rubber elephant.

Play Books for Toddlers & Preschoolers

Carle, Eric. *The Very Busy Spider*. Philomel, 1984. Farm animals try to keep a spider from spinning her web, but she doesn't give up and she makes a beautiful and useful creation. Pictures may be felt as well as seen, making this a great book for visually impaired children.

Hill, Eric. *Where's Spot?* Putnam, 1980. In an interactive lift-the-flap book, children help Spot's mother, Sally, search the house to find him. This book has been translated into a number of languages, including a sign language version.

Kunhardt, Dorothy. *Pat the Bunny*. Golden Books, 1990. In this touch-and-feel book, Paul and Judy smell the flowers, feel Daddy's scratchy face, look in the mirror, play peek-a-boo, and, of course, pat the bunny.

Lacome, Julie. *Seashore*. Candlewick, 1995. Small fingers can poke through the holes in the pages of this board book about the beach, and seem to change into fins, wings, or crawling legs.

Alphabet Books for Preschoolers to First-Graders

Kitamura, Satoshi. *From Acorn to Zoo and Everything in Between in Alphabetical Order*. Sunburst, 1995. Each page shows an assortment of things that begin with the same letter—all clearly labeled. For each page, there is a question (and a clue) that can be answered only by looking carefully at the picture.

MacDonald, Suse. *Alphabatics*. Bradbury Press, 1986. The letters of the alphabet are transformed and placed in 26 illustrations so that the hole in b becomes a balloon and y turns into the head of a yak (an ox with long hair).

Rankin, Laura. *The Handmade Alphabet*. Puffin, 1996. This book presents the handshape for each letter of the manual alphabet (American Sign Language) accompanied by an object whose name begins with that letter.

Shannon, George. *Tomorrow's Alphabet*. Mulberry Books, 1999. A is for seed—what's going on here? The seed is tomorrow's Apple! An imaginative alphabet puzzle that encourages children to think and make predictions.

Shelby, Anne. *Potluck*. Orchard, 1991. A multicultural collection of friends having names starting with A-Z bring a variety of dishes to a potluck.

Wordless Picture Books for Preschoolers to First-Graders

Carle, Eric. *Do You Want to Be My Friend?* HarperCollins, 1995. A little mouse asks all kinds of animals, "Do you want to be my friend?"

dePaola, Tomie. *Pancakes for Breakfast*. Voyager Books, 1990. A little old lady's attempts to have pancakes for breakfast are hindered by a lack of ingredients and the help of her pets.

Mayer, Mercer. *A Boy, a Dog, and a Frog*. Econo-Clad Books, 1999. A boy and a dog try unsuccessfully to catch a frog.

McCully, Emily. *School*. HarperTrophy, 1990. The eight oldest mice in a family prepare for the first day of school. After everyone leaves, and the house is too quiet, the youngest mouse decides to go discover what school is all about.

Wiesner, David. *Tuesday*. Clarion, 1991. One night a town is invaded by extraterrestrial frogs, flying in on their lily pads.

Rhyming Books for Toddlers to Kindergartners

Christelow, Eileen. *Five Little Monkeys Jumping on the Bed*. Clarion, 1989. This counting rhyme shows five little monkeys getting ready for bed and getting sidetracked by some serious bed-jumping.

Cole, Joanna, and Calmenson, Stephanie. *Eentsy, Weentsy Spider: Fingerplays and Action Rhymes*. Morrow, 1991. This book, illustrated using children of diverse cultural backgrounds, includes fingerplays and action rhymes that have been chanted, sung, and loved by generations.

Dyer, Jane. *Animal Crackers: A Delectable Collection of Pictures, Poems, and Lullabies for the Very Young*. Little, Brown, 1996. This picture book contains a collection of Mother Goose classics, modern poems, lullabies, and simple stories, many of which celebrate special times in a child's first years.

Martin, Bill, Jr., and Archambault, John. *Chicka Chicka Boom Boom*. Simon & Schuster, 1989. The rhythmical story of letters of the alphabet climbing and falling from a coconut tree.

"Predictable" Books for Toddlers to First-Graders

Aardema, Verna. *Bringing the Rain to Kapiti Plain*. Dutton, 1993. Told in verse, this is the story of how Ki-pat, a herder, makes it rain on the dry Kapiti Plain.

Hutchins, Pat. *Rosie's Walk*. Macmillan, 1968. Rosie the hen goes for a walk and manages to avoid many attempts on her life by a predatory fox. Also available in Spanish.

Lowell, Susan. *The Three Little Javelinas*. Northland Pub., 1993. This Southwestern tale, based on "The Three Little Pigs" and illustrated with Native American and Latino characters, is about three little javelinas as they try to outsmart the coyote who had hoped to eat them with red chili sauce.

Martin, Bill, Jr. *Brown Bear, Brown Bear, What Do You See?* Holt, 1996. What children see is a surprising cast of animals!

McNaughton, Colin. *Suddenly!* Harcourt Brace, 1995. Time after time, Preston the Pig outwits a hungry wolf that is trying to catch and eat him.

Multiple-Language Books for Preschoolers to First-Graders

Brown, Ruth. *Alphabet Times Four: An International ABC.* Dutton, 1991. Beginning with the letter A and ending with Z, this book offers a word that happens to begin with the same letter in four languages, English, Spanish, French, and German, accompanied by creatively bordered pictures.

Garza, Carmen Lomas. *Family Pictures.* Children's Book Press, 1990. In this bilingual text (Spanish and English), a young girl remembers her day-to-day family life while growing up in Texas in a Mexican-American culture.

Hirschi, Ron. *Seya's Song.* Sasquatch Books, 1992. A young S'Klallam girl follows the seasons of the salmon, interweaving aspects of the life and culture of her Pacific Coast tribe and using words from her native language.

Lee, Huy Voun. *In the Park.* Henry Holt & Co, Inc., 1998. Xiao Ming and his mother go to the park, where they see a variety of people of different cultures, ages, and disabilities. At the park, his mother teaches him how to draw and pronounce some Chinese characters.

Rattigan, Jama Kim. *Dumpling Soup.* Little, Brown, 1993. Marisa, a 7-year-old girl who lives in Hawaii, explains the traditions her family celebrates at the New Year. Hawaiian, Japanese, and Korean words and phrases add to the English text.

Stock, Catherine. *Where Are You Going Manyoni?* Morrow, 1993. Manyoni lives in Zimbabwe and on her way to school she passes many beautiful areas, wild animals, and birds. The book includes a picture glossary of wildlife and a key to pronouncing African words.

Beginning Readers

Eastman, P. D. *Go, Dog. Go!* Random House, 1989. Big dogs, little dogs—black, white, yellow, and blue dogs—they're all very busy going places and doing things.

Krauss, Ruth. *The Carrot Seed*. Harper Collins, 1973. A little boy knows a carrot will grow from the seed that he planted, no matter what anyone else may say or think.

Read-Aloud Chapter Books for Preschoolers to First-Graders

Cameron, Ann. *The Stories Julian Tells*. Knopf, 1981. Julian tells great stories. He can make people, especially his younger brother Huey, believe almost anything, which sometimes leads to lots of trouble.

Milne, A. A. *The House at Pooh Corner*. Dutton, 1991. The book is about the timeless adventures of Pooh, Piglet, Christopher Robin, Owl, Tigger, and Eeyore in the Hundred-Acre Woods.

CHILDREN'S MAGAZINES

Babybug

P.O. Box 9304

LaSalle, IL 61301-9897

(http://www.babybugmag.com)

Board-book magazine, with illustrated rhymes and stories for parents to read with children. (Ages 6 months to 2 years)

Click!

P.O. Box 9304

LaSalle, IL 61301-9897

(http://www.clickmag.com)

Contains science and social studies stories, both informational and fiction. (Ages 5-6)

Sesame Street Magazine

Children's Television Workshop

One Lincoln Plaza

New York, NY 10023

(http://www.ctw.org/sesame/)

Sesame Street characters are featured in stories, poems, puzzles, posters, and more. (Ages 2-6)

Your Big Back Yard

National Wildlife Federation

8925 Leesburg Pike

Vienna, VA 22184

(http://www.nwf.org/yourbigbackyard)

Includes stories, poems, riddles, and games, with color pictures of animals.

COMPUTER PROGRAMS

Living Books: Interactive Animated Stories
(Ages 3-7)

These programs provide a place for children to hear a story, read along with the narrator, or read by themselves. They also can interact with characters and objects and play games that teach the alphabet, simple words, rhyming, and other reading skills. Each program also comes with the matching book. Some examples of titles:

— ***Just Grandma and Me***
— ***The Cat and the Hat***
— ***Arthur's Birthday***
— ***Dr. Seuss's ABC***

Many include versions in Spanish, French, and German along with the English text.

For more information, contact:

Broderbund Software, Inc.
Toll Free: 1-800-567-2610
http://www.broderbund.com/

Bailey's Book House
(Ages 2-5)

This software features Bailey and his friends as they encourage young children to build literacy skills and develop a love for reading. It includes activities to help youngsters explore letters, words, sentences, rhyming, and stories. No reading skills are required; all directions are spoken.

Let's Go Read! An Island Adventure
(Ages 4-7)

Children join Robby Raccoon and his friends in their adventures on an island inhabited by the alphabet. Included are activities to help children learn reading basics, like letter sounds, and how to sound out and build simple words. Children can command the computer with their voices, and record and listen to themselves reading.

For more information, including Spanish titles and a catalog for children with special needs, contact:

Riverdeep
Toll Free: 1-800-362-2890
http://www.riverdeep.net/edmark/

Young Children and the Internet: Places to Learn and Play

Arthur: http://www.pbs.org/wgbh/pages/arthur/

Barney: http://www.barney.com

Disney: http://www.disney.com

Dr. Seuss's Seussville: http://www.randomhouse.com/seussville/

PBS Homepage: http://www.pbs.org/kids/

Children's Television Workshop: http://www.ctw.org

Smithsonian Institution—National Zoo: http://nationalzoo.si.edu/

RESOURCES FOR PARENTS

The resources below are primarily for parents, but you can use them to guide you to resources for your children as well. Many of the books include excellent children's book lists; two are outstanding anthologies*. In addition, don't overlook your public library as a source of book lists for children. Many publish their own lists of books that may relate to special programs for children or community needs and events.

Butler, Dorothy. *Babies Need Books, 2nd edition*. Atheneum.

Cullinan, Bernice. *Read to Me: Raising Kids Who Love to Read*. Scholastic, Inc.

*Fadiman, Clifton, ed. *The World Treasury of Children's Literature*. Little, Brown and Company.

Graves, Ruth, ed. *The RIF Guide to Encouraging Young Readers*. Doubleday. (RIF = Reading Is Fundamental, Inc.)

Hearne, Betsy. *Choosing Books for Children*. Delacorte Press.

Kimmel, Margaret Mary. *For Reading Out Loud: A Guide to Sharing Books with Children*. Delacorte Press.

Larrick, Nancy. *A Parent's Guide to Children's Reading, 5th edition*. Bantam Books.

*Russell, William F., ed. *Classics to Read Aloud to Your Children, 1984 edition*. Crown.

Sader, Marion. *Reference Books for Young Readers: Authoritative Evaluations of Encyclopedias, Atlases, and Dictionaries*. Bowker.

Trelease, Jim. *The New Read-Aloud Handbook*. Penguin Handbooks.

In Addition

The organizations below also publish lists of children's books and other helpful brochures that are available free or at a nominal cost, and books for parents on helping children learn to read. Request titles and ordering information directly from:

American Library Association
Publications Order Department
50 East Huron Street
Chicago, IL 60611

International Reading Association
800 Barksdale Road
P.O. Box 8139
Newark, DE 19714-8139

Reading Is Fundamental, Inc.
Publications Department Smithsonian Institution
600 Maryland Avenue, SW, Suite 500
Washington, DC 20024-2520

Federal Sources of Assistance If Your Child Has a Reading Problem or Learning Disability

ERIC Clearinghouse on Disabilities and Gifted Children
The Council for Exceptional Children
1920 Association Drive
Reston, VA 20191

National Information Center for Children and Youth with Disabilities
P.O. Box 1492
Washington, DC 20013-1492

National Institute of Child Health and Human Development
U.S. Department of Health and Human Services
9000 Rockville Pike, Bldg. 31
Bethesda, MD 20892

The National Library Service for the Blind and Physically Handicapped
Library of Congress
Washington, DC 20542   (202) 702-5100

Office of Special Education and Rehabilitative Services
U.S. Department of Education
Washington, DC 20202

Federal Publications for Parents on Helping Your Child

In addition to *Helping Your Child Learn to Read*, the U.S. Department of Education publishes a number of books on related subjects. To find out what's available and how to order, request the Consumer Information Catalog listing nearly 200 useful federal publications. The Catalog is free from the Consumer Information Center, Pueblo, Colorado 81009.

Resources – Author's Picks

CHILDREN'S BOOKS

Babies (Board Books)

Berenstain, Jan and Stan. *The Berenstain Bears Inside Outside Upside Down*. Random House, 1997. Little Bear travels to town inside a cardboard box. (Bright and Early Book Series)

Boynton, Sandra. *Moo, Baa, La La La*. Simon & Schuster, 1982. This is a fun rhyming book with brilliant illustrations and animal sounds for you to make.

Brown, Margaret Wise. *The Runaway Bunny*. HarperCollins, 2005. A little bunny keeps running away from his mother in an imaginative game of verbal hide-and-seek. Children will be profoundly comforted by this lovingly steadfast mother who finds her child every time.

Carle, Eric. *Little Cloud*. Putnam, 2001. This sweet story about a cloud changing shape will inspire the imagination.

Carle, Eric. *The Very Hungry Caterpillar*. Philomel, 2007. Children will be fascinated by the caterpillar's varied diet and miraculous transformation into a beautiful butterfly.

Carle, Eric. *The Very Quiet Cricket*. Philomel, 1990. Your child will delight in the surprise at the end of the book and in knowing that every creature can find its voice, however silent or joyous.

Cousins, Lucy. *Maisy's Favorite Animals*. Candlewick Press, 2001. Maisy has fun playing with her animals and toys. (Maisy Series)

Day, Alexandra. *Carl's Afternoon in the Park*. HarperCollins, 1992. Follow baby and puppy as they tour around the park with big dog, Carl. (Carl Board Book Series)

Degen, Bruce. *Jamberry*. HarperCollins, 1995. Go on a berry-picking adventure with a boy and a bear in this fun-filled rhyming storybook. (I Can Read Series)

Diehl, David. *Sports A to Z*. Lark Books NC, 2007. Learn about different sports while learning your ABCs.

DK Publishing. *All About Me!* DK Publishing, 2008. This lift-the-flap board book teaches babies about the different parts of their bodies. (Fun Flaps)

Dorling Kindersley. *Touch and Feel Baby Animals*. DK Publishing, 1999. Touch and feel the different textures in this sweet book about baby animals. (Touch and Feel Series)

Dorling Kindersley. *Touch and Feel Home*. DK Publishing, 1998. Touch and feel the different textures in this sweet book about everyday items found at home.

Eastman, P.D. *Big Dog, Little Dog*. Random House Children's Books, 2006. Fred and Ted are two dogs who are best friends, even though just about everything about them is opposite. (Bright and Early Board Book Series)

Martin Jr., Bill. *Panda Bear, Panda Bear, What Do You See?* Henry Holt & Company, Inc., 2006. See ten different endangered animals in this beautifully illustrated board book drawn by Eric Carle.

Marzollo, Jean. *I Spy Little Animals*. Scholastic, 1998. Use picture clues to find animals and more on each page of this eye-catching rhyming book. (I Spy Series)

Marzollo, Jean. *I Spy Little Book*. Scholastic, 1998. Use picture clues to find hidden treasures on each page of this wonderful rhyming book. (I Spy Series)

Marzollo, Jean. *I Spy Little Wheels*. Scholastic, 1997. Use picture clues to find little vehicles on each page of this creative rhyming book. (I Spy Series)

McCue, Lisa. *Corduroy's Day*. Viking Penguin, 2005. Count to 10 with Corduroy as he goes throughout his day. (Corduroy Series)

McCue, Lisa. *Corduroy's Party*. Viking Penguin, 2005. Come along with Corduroy as he gets ready for his birthday party. (Corduroy Series)

Oxenbury, Helen. *I See*. Candlewick Press, 1995. Follow a small child for the day to see what he sees, in soft colors and simple text. (Baby Beginner Board Book Series)

Oxenbury, Helen. *I Touch*. Candlewick Press, 1995. Follow a small child for the day to see what he touches, in soft colors and simple text. (Baby Beginner Board Book Series)

Patricelli, Leslie. *No No Yes Yes*. Candlewick, 2008. An expressive baby demonstrates familiar behaviors—and their predictable responses—in an amusing board book.

Patricelli, Leslie. *Quiet Loud*. Candlewick, 2003. Learning about opposites has never been more fun—or funny—than with this spirited board book.

Perkins, Al. *Dr. Seuss's ABC*. Random House, 1996. Learn your ABCs with this wonderful Dr. Seuss board book. (Bright and Early Board Book Series)

Perkins, Al. *Hand, Hand, Fingers, Thumb.* Random House, 1998. Find your way rhyming through a sea of monkeys as they play musical instruments with their hands, fingers, and thumbs. (Bright and Early Board Book Series)

Rosen, Michael. *We're Going on a Bear Hunt.* Simon & Schuster Children's Publishing, 1997. Follow a family as they go through the grass, a river, some mud, a forest, and even a snowstorm, and then go back quickly after they encounter a bear. (Classic Board Books)

Ross, Katharine. *The Little Quiet Book.* Random House, 2002. A very peaceful and quiet book.

Toys, Alex. *Mother Goose Rhymes.* Little, Brown Books for Young Readers, 2007. This is a wonderful nursery rhyme book, with four detachable finger puppets and a felt board.

Verdick, Elizabeth. *Teeth Are Not for Biting.* Free Spirit Publishing, Inc., 2003. Babies and toddlers learn about getting along with others and expressing their feelings in ways other than biting. (Best Behavior Series)

Watt, Fiona. *That's Not My Puppy.* EDC Publishing, 2000. Bright colors, fun illustrations, and rhyming text make this book a child favorite. (Touchy Feely Series)

Toddlers & Preschool

Browne, Anthony. *Things I Like.* Dragonfly Books, 1989. A little monkey shows us some of his favorite things.

Browne, Anthony. *I Like Books.* Walker Books Ltd, 2003. A little monkey shows us all the different types of books he likes.

Heller, Lora. *Baby Fingers: I Want...Teaching Your Baby to Sign.* Sterling Publishing, 2006. Help your baby or toddler learn to communicate with these vivid photographs of children signing.

Piper, Watty. *The Little Engine That Could*. Penguin Young Readers Group, 2005. Despite its size, the Little Engine That Could is able to pull its load of toys over the mountain for all the girls and boys waiting on the other side.

Rhyming Books for Toddlers & Up

Alborough, Jez. *My Friend Bear*. Candlewick Press, 2001. Eddie's stuffed bear is too big to hold, and the real bear he meets has a toy bear that's too small. Could they have been switched?

Appelt, Kathi. *Incredible Me!* HarperCollins, 2003. A girl celebrates her own individuality, from her freckles to her wiggles.

Black, Sonia. *Plenty of Penguins*. Scholastic, Inc., 2000. Learn all about penguins in this early reader rhyming book. (Scholastic's Hello Reader! Science Series)

Bryan Cauley, Lorinda. *Clap Your Hands*. Penguin Young Readers Group, 1997. Get your kids up jumping, hopping, spinning, and more with this active rhyming book.

Carter, David. *Birthday Bugs*. Simon and Schuster Children's Publishing, 2004. Celebrate with the Birthday Bugs as they pop out of birthday presents, and there's even a birthday hat for you to wear so you can be a Birthday Bug too!

Cobb, Annie. *Wheels!* Random House Children's Books, 1996. This predictable rhyming book is one of the many wonderful books in the "Early Step into Reading" book series for preschool and kindergarten.

Curtis, Jamie Lee. *Big Words for Little People*. HarperCollins, 2008. A boisterous and zany family celebrates the power of language and discovers that words – big or little – are the bridge that connects us all.

Curtis, Jamie Lee. *I'm Gonna Like Me: Letting Off a Little Self-Esteem*. HarperCollins, 2002. A delightful book about accepting ourselves with all of our strengths and weaknesses.

Curtis, Jamie Lee. *Is There Really a Human Race?* HarperCollins, 2006. Is the human race an obstacle course? Is it a sprint? Do we get our own lane? Great questions to ponder in this clever book about some of life's choices.

Curtis, Jamie Lee. *It's Hard to Be Five: Learning How to Work My Control Panel*. HarperCollins, 2004. This book helps to make the struggles of a five-year-old's self-control a little bit easier, and a lot more fun!

Curtis, Jamie Lee. *Today I Feel Silly & Other Moods That Make My Day*. HarperCollins, 1998. A child's emotions range from silliness to anger to excitement, coloring and changing each day.

Curtis, Jamie Lee. *Where Do Balloons Go? An Uplifting Mystery*. HarperCollins, 2000. Written in rhyme, this witty and imaginative story will amuse children as they explore the possibilities of what might happen after you let go of a balloon.

Dorfman, Craig. *I Knew You Could!: Celebrate All the Stops in Your Life*. Grosset & Dunlap, 2008. A journey with "The Little Engine That Could" through some of life's peaks and valleys, with encouraging words of determination and wisdom.

Dr. Seuss. *Did I Ever Tell You How Lucky You Are?* Random House, 1973. Children will be happy just contemplating the outrageous array of troubles they're lucky they don't have.

What Children Need to Learn to READ

Dr. Seuss. *One Fish Two Fish Red Fish Blue Fish*. Random House, 1960. Children will be entranced by these ridiculous and fun rhymes.

Dr. Seuss. *The Cat in the Hat*. Random House, 1957. The classic story of the cat who transformed a dull, rainy afternoon into a messy yet magical and exciting adventure.

Dr. Seuss. *The Foot Book: Dr. Seuss's Wacky Book of Opposites*. Random House Children's Books, 1996. Learn about opposites in this fun-filled rhyming book by Dr. Seuss. (Bright and Early Book Series)

Dr. Seuss. *The Sneetches and Other Stories*. Random House, 1961. Children will appreciate the wacky illustrations and silly yet thought-provoking prose.

Dr. Seuss. *There's a Wocket in my Pocket*. Random House Children's Books, 1996. A young boy finds many wonderful creatures with names that rhyme with objects and rooms around his house. (Bright and Early Book Series)

Dr. Seuss. *Wacky Wednesday*. Random House, 1974. A baffled youngster awakens one morning to find everything's out of place, but no one else seems to notice.

Evans, Lezlie. *Rain Song*. Houghton Mifflin Company, 1995. See what fun a rainy day can truly be in this eloquent rhyming book.

Fleming, Maria. *Jumping Jill Went Down the Hill*. Scholastic, Inc., 2002. Learn about the "ill" sound in this humorous tale about Jill. (Word Family Tales Series)

Peet, Bill. *The Caboose Who Got Loose*. Houghton Mifflin Company, 1980. Katy Caboose is always the last car on the train. Something happens and she finally gets her dream of peace and quiet. This is a wonderful classic story, and its words are almost melodic.

Perkins, Al. *The Digging-est Dog*. Random House, 1967. A dog that has learned to dig doesn't stop until he has dug up the whole town!

Pomerantz, Charlotte. *The Piggy in the Puddle*. Simon and Schuster Children's Publishing, 1989. This sing-song book is so much fun to read. A little piggy doesn't want to leave her fun in the mud puddle. Her family all try to persuade her to come out. Then one by one, they all give in and join in the fun.

Prelutsky, Jack. *Read-Aloud Rhymes for the Very Young*. Random House Children's Books, 1986. What a combination—Jack Prelutsky's selected rhymes, with pictures created by Marc Brown, illustrator of the "Arthur" book and television series.

Regan, Dana. *Monkey See, Monkey Do*. Penguin Young Readers Group, 2000. Monkeys sure can have lots of fun! Rhyme your way through a day with these crazy creatures. (All Aboard Reading Series)

Wells, Rosemary. *Read to Your Bunny*. Scholastic Inc., 2003. This short picture book is quite a gem. Both you and your child will love this book, and will be encouraged to enjoy reading together.

Predictable Books for Toddlers & Up

Berry, Holly. *Old MacDonald Had a Farm*. North-South/Night Sky Books, 1997. The traditional song is beautifully illustrated in this book.

Carle, Eric. *Do You Want to Be My Friend?* Penguin Group, 1988. A little mouse asks many different animals to be his friend, and finally finds one in the end.

Dale, Penny. *Ten in the Bed*. Candlewick Press, 2007. Count down from 10 to 1, as all the stuffed animals fall out of the bed.

Hillenbrand, Will. *Down by the Station*. Harcourt Children's Books, 2002. Follow along with a train that picks up all sorts of animals on its journey and makes fun sound effects along the way.

Murphy, Stuart J. *Beep Beep, Vroom Vroom*. San Val, Incorporated, 2000. Molly loves to play with her big brother's toy cars. Every other page has a repetitive phrase that your child will enjoy saying along with you. The book also helps to teach the mathematical concept of patterns. Molly has to try to line the cars up by color, just before her brother comes back.

Zelinsky, Paul. *The Wheels on the Bus*. Penguin Young Readers Group, 1990. Along with the song, "Wheels on the Bus," this book also includes moveable parts that make the experience even more interactive.

Alphabet Books

Amery, Heather. *Usborne Farmyard Tales Alphabet Book*. EDC Publishing, 1998. In this book, you will find an alphabet letter showcased on each page, with pictures of things that start with that letter. In addition, at the bottom of each page there is a question to answer and a complete list of the alphabet letters, with the showcased letter highlighted.

Base, Graeme. *Animalia*. Harry N. Abrams, Inc., 1987. This is a beautifully illustrated alphabet book. Each letter is paired with an animal and displays an alliterative phrase. There are many other hidden objects to find within each picture.

Beall, Pamela Conn. *ABC (Wee Sing and Learn)*. Penguin Young Readers Group, 2000. This 32-page book and 20-minute cassette help children playfully learn their letters and sounds through music and song.

Carlson, Nancy. *ABC I Like Me!* Penguin Group (USA) Inc., 1999. Help build your child's self-esteem while learning the alphabet with this vibrant ABC book.

Chin, Oliver Clyde. *The Adventures of Wonderbaby: From A to Z*. Immedium, 2008. Have fun with this hilariously wacky alphabet board book.

Funfax. *My Big Alphabet Book*. DK Publishing, Inc., 1999. This large board book has tabs to mark pages on which you can learn about the different letters of the alphabet.

Martin Jr., Bill. *Chicka Chicka Boom Boom*. Simon and Schuster Children's Publishing, 2000. This is a fun rhyming alphabet book, with repetitive phrases that kids love to join in and say. The letters each try to climb up the coconut tree and hope there is "enough room."

Melmed, Laura Krauss. *New York: The Big Apple from A – Z*. HarperCollins Children's Books, 2005. See New York in all its glory, from its busy neighborhoods to its fascinating historical locations, its parks, its buildings, and more—all from A to Z.

Pallotta, Jerry. *Ocean Alphabet Book*. Charlesbridge Publishing, Inc., 1989. Learn about letters throughout the depths of the ocean.

Priddy, Roger. *Bright Baby Colors, ABC, Numbers*. Priddy Bicknell Books, 2008. Babies learn about colors, ABCs and numbers in this brightly illustrated board book.

Scarry, Richard. *Richard Scarry's Cars and Trucks from A to Z*. Random House Children's Books, 1990. Learn your alphabet with Richard Scarry's whimsically unique vehicles.

Smith, R. M. *An A to Z Walk in the Park (Animal Alphabet Book)*. Clarence Henry Books, 2008. Children learn their ABCs and learn about over 200 different animals in the pages of this alphabet book.

Preschool & Up

Barrett, Judi. *Cloudy With a Chance of Meatballs*. Simon and Schuster Children's Publishing, 1982. What would it be like if food came down from the sky? The weather forecasts are sure strange in the town of Chewandswallow.

Berenstain, Stan & Jan. *The Berenstain Bears and the Big Road Race*. Random House Children's Books, 1987. Just like the tortoise in the Tortoise and the Hare story, Brother Bear ends up winning the race. (Berenstain Bears Series)

Bourgeois, Paulette. *Franklin's Class Trip*. Kids Can Press, Limited, 1999. Franklin is excited about going on his class trip to the museum, until he hears about the dinosaurs. Find out how Franklin does at the museum. (Franklin Series)

Brett, Jan. *The Mitten*. Penguin Group (USA), 1996. After Nicki drops his white mitten in the snow, woodland animals climb in, one by one, starting from the smallest animal to very large animals.

Bridwell, Norman. *Clifford at the Circus*. Scholastic, Inc., 1985. Clifford starts out trying to save the circus and ends up having to rescue Emily Elizabeth. (Clifford Series)

Brown, Marc. *Glasses for D.W.* Random House Children's Books, 1996. D.W. tries to convince Arthur that she needs glasses, just like he does. (Arthur Adventure Series)

Carlson, Nancy. *I Like Me!* Puffin, 1990. By admiring her finer points and showing that she can have fun even when there's no one else around, a charming pig proves the best friend you can have is yourself.

Cronin, Doreen. *Diary of a Fly*. HarperCollins, 2007. A young fly realizes that there is a lot to learn about mastering flight school and getting along with 327 brothers and sisters. He also discovers that heroes come in all shapes and sizes.

Cronin, Doreen. *Diary of a Spider*. HarperCollins, 2005. A young spider discovers that there is a lot to learn about being a spider, including how to spin webs and avoid vacuum cleaners.

Cronin, Doreen. *Diary of a Worm*. HarperCollins, 2003. A young worm discovers that there are some very good and some not so good things about being a worm in this great, big world.

Freeman, Don. *Corduroy*. Viking, 1968. A sweet, little bear named Corduroy has lost a button on his overalls. He searches all over a big department store to find it. In the end, he finds something even better than a button. He finds a friend. (Corduroy Series)

Joffe Numeroff, Laura. *If You Give a Cat a Cupcake*. HarperCollins Publishers, 2008. Giving the cat an innocent little cupcake starts an avalanche of requests that keep the child in the story very busy indeed.

Joffe Numeroff, Laura. *If You Give a Moose a Muffin*. HarperCollins Publishers, 1991. A little boy does everything he can think of to entertain this funny moose, who never seems to be satisfied.

Joffe Numeroff, Laura. *If You Give a Mouse a Cookie*. HarperCollins Publishers, 1985. A young boy starts out by giving a mouse a cookie, and then has to cater to his new friend's every whim.

Joffe Numeroff, Laura. *If You Give a Pig a Pancake*. HarperCollins Children's Books, 1998. Once the young girl in the story gives the pig a pancake, the pig keeps her busy with request after request.

Johnson, Crockett. *Harold and the Purple Crayon*. HarperCollins, 1998. While out for a walk, a small boy draws himself some amazing adventures with his crayon.

Joyce, William. *George Shrinks*. HarperCollins Children's Books, 1987. Being only 3 inches tall would be a challenge for anyone. The adventurous George Shrinks seems to handle it well.

Kasza, Keiko. *A Mother for Choco*. Penguin Group (USA) Incorporated, 1996. This is a heartwarming story about a little bird named Choco who is looking for her mother. She searches high and low until she is taken in by Mrs. Bear, whose other children are Pig, Hippo, and Alligator. Families come in all different shapes and sizes.

Kennedy, Jimmy. *The Teddy Bears' Picnic*. Simon and Schuster Children's Publishing, 2000. A group of young children come across a party of teddy bears out in the woods having a wonderfully magical picnic.

London, Jonathan. *Let's Go Froggy!* Penguin Group (USA) Incorporated, 1996. Froggy is going bike riding with his dad, but takes forever to get ready to go. (Froggy Series)

Mayer, Mercer. *Beach Day, Vol. 1*. School Specialty Children's Publishing, 2001. Little Critter and his sister spend the day at the beach with their dad. This is one of the books in the First Reader's Skills and Practice Series. (Little Critter Series)

Mayer, Mercer. *Just Me and My Little Brother*. Random House Children's Books, 1998. Little Critter can't wait to do all sorts of fun things with his little brother. But first, his little brother has to learn how to walk. (Little Critter Series)

Mayer, Mercer. *Just Me and My Mom*. Random House Children's Books, 2001. Little Critter has quite an adventure spending the day with his mom. (Little Critter Series)

McDonnell, Patrick. *The Gift of Nothing*. Little, Brown, 2005. Mooch the cat wants to give his best friend, Earl the dog, a gift. But what do you give to someone who has everything?

Munson, Derek. *Enemy Pie*. Chronicle Books LLC, 2000. A little boy hopes that the enemy pie that his dad makes for him will help him get rid of his enemy, but instead, he makes a new friend.

Rey, Margaret. *Curious George and the Dump Truck*. Houghton Mifflin Company, 1999. Curious George gets into trouble again. Watch him as he tries to find a creative solution to his problems. (Curious George Series)

Sendak, Maurice. *Where the Wild Things Are*. HarperCollins Publishers, 1991. Max is sent to his room without his supper for misbehaving. His room turns into a jungle and Max is off on an exciting adventure.

Silverstein, Shel. *The Giving Tree*. HarperCollins, 2004. Every day the boy would come to the tree to eat her apples, swing from her branches, or slide down her trunk… and the tree was happy. But as the boy grew older, he began to want more from the tree, and the tree gave and gave.

Stevens, Janet. *My Big Dog*. Golden Books, 2005. Merl the cat tries everything to get rid of the new dog. Can a cat and dog finally learn to be friends?

Stoutland, Allison. *Reach for the Sky: And Other Little Lessons for a Happier World*. Inch By Inch Publications, 1999. As inspiring as it is fun, this book offers the message that every person can make a difference with his or her unique qualities.

Van Allsburg, Chris. *Two Bad Ants*. Houghton Mifflin, 1998. When two ants desert their colony, they experience an adventure that convinces them to return home.

Willems, Mo. *Don't Let the Pigeon Drive the Bus!* Hyperion Press, 2003. Would you let this funny and conniving pigeon drive the bus?

Willems, Mo. *Don't Let the Pigeon Stay Up Late!* Hyperion, 2006. It's getting dark, but the pigeon won't go to bed! Will you let him stay up late?

Willems, Mo. *The Pigeon Finds a Hot Dog!* Hyperion, 2004. When Pigeon finds a hot dog, he can't wait to shove the entire thing into his beak. But then a very sly duckling enters the scene and wants a bite. Who will be the more clever bird?

Beginning Reader Books & Book Series

Alder, Anita A. *Young Cam Jansen and the Baseball Mystery*. Penguin Young Readers Group, 2001. Before the kids can play, they need to find their missing baseball. Cam tries to use her photographic memory to solve the mystery. (Young Cam Jansen Series)

Benjamin, Ruth. *My Little Pony: Sleepover Surprise*. HarperCollins Children's Books, 2005. This sweet book has picture words interspersed throughout to encourage children to become involved in the reading process (rebus story). (My Little Pony Series)

Clarke, Ginjer. *Cheetah Cubs*. Penguin Group (USA), 2007. Learn all about cheetahs in this informative animal book. (All Aboard Science Reader Series)

Earhart, Kristin. *The Magic School Bus Gets Crabby*. Scholastic, Inc., 2006. Learning about tide pools has never been more fun than in this adventurous encounter with crabs and more. (Magic School Bus Series)

Hoff, Syd. *Danny and the Dinosaur*. HarperCollins Children's Books, 2008. Danny has fun with a dinosaur he meets in the museum. They have lots of adventures together until the dinosaur has to go back to the museum. (I Can Read Book 1 Series)

Holmelund Minarik, Else. *Little Bear*. HarperCollins Publishers, 1992. This classic book contains three heartwarming short stories about Little Bear and his mom. (I Can Read Series)

Inches, Alison. *The Big Itch*. Scholastic, Inc., 2003. Clifford's scratching is causing "big" problems. What can Emily Elizabeth do to help Clifford and stop his itch? (Clifford Big Red Reading Series)

Laurence, Daniel. *Captain and Matey Set Sail*. HarperCollins Children's Books, 2002. This beginning chapter book is about two silly pirates who set sail on the high seas. As they search for buried treasure, they find out that the true treasure is their friendship.

Lobel, Arnold. *Frog and Toad Together*. HarperCollins Publishers, 1979. This classic Newberry Honor book has entertained many children over the years and is a great beginning chapter book. (I Can Read Series)

Maccarone, Grace. *First Grade Friends Forever!* Scholastic, Inc., 2006. This book includes six different stories about the adventures of the kids in the first grade class.

Parish, Peggy. *Play Ball, Amelia Bedelia*. HarperCollins Publishers, 1995. Amelia Bedelia takes everything literally. Have fun watching her try to play baseball on the team. (I Can Read Series)

Pilkey, Dav. *Dogzilla*. Harcourt Paperbacks, 2003. The town of Mousopolis is temporarily taken over by an overgrown dog in this unique and hilarious story.

Preller, James. *Hiccups for Elephant*. Scholastic, Inc., 1995. Have you ever had the hiccups? All the animals have ideas for elephant to try to stop his hiccups. (Hello Reader! Series)

Royston, Angela. *Truck Trouble*. Topeka Bindery, 1998. Learn about trucks as you follow John on his deliveries in his big rig. John seems to have a bit of trouble along the way. (DK Readers Series, Level 1)

Rylant, Cynthia. *Henry and Mudge, The First Book*. Simon & Schuster Children's Publishing, 1996. Mudge is Henry's beloved big dog, and best friend. This wonderful book is in the Ready-to-Read books series. (Henry and Mudge Series)

Rylant, Cynthia. *Henry and Mudge and the Forever Sea*. Simon & Schuster Children's Publishing, 1997. Henry and Mudge spend an adventurous day together at the beach, in this beginning chapter book. (Henry and Mudge Series)

Weinman Sharmat, Marjorie. *Nate the Great and the Boring Beach Bag*. Random House Children's Books, 1989. Nate the Great has another mystery to solve. This time he is trying to find Oliver's beach bag. (Nate the Great Series)

Next Level Chapter Books for Read Aloud & More Advanced Readers

Brown, Marc. *Arthur and the Race to Read*. Little, Brown Books for Young Readers, 2008. Arthur and his friends are getting ready for a running race to earn money for literacy. (Arthur Chapter Book Series, #1)

Dadey, Debbie. *Cupid Doesn't Flip Hamburgers*. Scholastic, Inc., 1995. The Bailey School Kids want to find out whether the new cook in the school cafeteria is really Cupid. (Adventures of the Bailey School Kids Series)

Danziger, Paula. *Amber Brown Is Not a Crayon*. Penguin Group (USA), 2006. Amber and Justin are best friends until they start to fight right before Justin has to move away. Will they get everything worked out in time? (Amber Brown Series)

Kline, Suzy. *Horrible Harry Goes to Sea*. Penguin Young Readers Group, 2003. Miss Mackle's class is taking a riverboat ride to see what it was like to sail the seas like their ancestors did. (Horrible Harry Series)

Malcolm, Jahnna N. *The Jewel Kingdom*. Backpack Books, 2006. Four princesses rule a magical land. This volume contains four books from the very popular series, The Jewel Kingdom.

Park, Barbara. *Junie B. Jones and her Big Fat Mouth*. Random House Children's Books, 1993. The Junie B. Jones books are "laugh-out-loud funny"! Watch as Junie B. tries to get the "bestest job" in her kindergarten class. (Junie B. Jones Series)

Peterson, John. *The Littles to the Rescue*. Topeka Bindery, 1993. The family of little people travel through a snowstorm to find Aunt Lily and help out with the birth of a new baby. (Littles Series)

Pilkey, Dav. *The Adventures of Captain Underpants*. Scholastic, Inc., 1997. Two friends write their own comic books and Captain Underpants comes to life. The hilarious books in this series will keep your child begging for more reading time. (Captain Underpants Series)

Pope Osborne, Mary. *Dinosaurs Before Dark*. Random House Children's Books, 1992. Jack and Annie are transported from their magic tree house to the time of the dinosaurs. (Magic Tree House Series, #1)

Preller, James. *The Case of the Runaway Dog*. Scholastic, Inc., 1999. Jigsaw and Mila are looking for clues to solve the mystery and find Jigsaw's missing dog, Rags. (Jigsaw Jones Mystery Series, #7)

Roy, Ron. *The Absent Author*. Random House Children's Books, 1997. The kids' favorite mystery author has been kidnapped. Can they help to solve the mystery before his scheduled visit to their school? (A to Z Mystery Series, #1)

West, Tracey. *Sprite's Secret*. Scholastic, Inc., 2000. Violet and her new fairy friend, Sprite, have to work together to save the day. (Pixie Tricks Series, #1)

What Children Need to Learn to READ

Children's Cookbooks

American Cancer Society Staff. *Kids' First Cookbook: Delicious-Nutritious Treats to Make Yourself!* McGraw Hill Companies, 2006.

Beery, Barbara. *Batter Up Kids: Delicious Desserts Sweet Treats from the Premier Children's Cooking School.* Gibbs Smith, 2004.

Beery, Barbara. *Fairies Cookbook.* Gibbs Smith, 2007.

Beery, Barbara. *Mermaid Cookbook.* Gibbs Smith, 2008.

Beery, Barbara. *Pink Princess Cookbook.* Gibbs Smith, 2006.

Better Homes and Gardens Editors. *Better Homes and Gardens Junior Cookbook.* Meredith Books, 2004.

Brennan, Georgeanne. *Green Eggs and Ham Cookbook.* Random House Childrens Books, 2006.

Crocker, Betty. *Betty Crocker Kids Cook!* Wiley, John & Sons, Incorporated, 2007.

Deen, Paula. *Paula Deen's My First Cookbook.* Simon and Schuster Children's Publishing, 2008.

DK Publishing. *Kids' Fun and Healthy Cookbook.* DK Publishing, 2007.

Dorling Kindersley Publishing Staff. *DK Children's Cookbook.* Dorling Kindersley Publishing, Incorporated, 2004.

Gold, Rozanne. *Kids Cook 1-2-3: Recipes for Young Chefs Using Only 3 Ingredients.* Bloomsbury USA, 2006.

Gooseberry Patch. *Kids in the Kitchen Cookbook: Recipes for Fun.* Gooseberry Patch, 2007.

Joffe Numeroff, Laura. *Mouse Cookies and More: A Treasury.* Harpercollins Childrens Books, 2006.

Johnson, Becky. *Baking with Tiny Tots: Over 50 Easy Recipes That You and Your Child Can Make Together*. Hamlyn, 2007.

Karmel, Annabel. *Mom and Me Cookbook: Have Fun in the Kitchen*. DK Publishing, Inc., 2005.

Karmel, Annabel. *The Toddler Cookbook*. DK Publishing, Inc., 2008.

Karpinski, Stephanie. *Magic Kitchen Cookbook*. Meredith Books, 2007.

Katzen, Mollie. *Pretend Soup and Other Real Recipes: A Cookbook for Preschoolers and Up*. Ten Speed Press, 1994.

Keller, Thomas. *What's Cooking?: A Cookbook for Kids*. Disney Press, 2007.

Kindersley, Dorling. *I Can Cook!* Dorling Kindersley Publishing, Incorporated, 2007.

Lagasse, Emeril. *Emeril's There's a Chef in My Soup!: Recipes for the Kid in Everyone*. HarperCollins Childrens Books, 2002.

McQuillan, Susan. *Sesame Street, C Is for Cooking: Recipes from the Street*. Wiley, John & Sons, Incorporated, 2007.

Nissenberg, Sandra K. *The Everything Kids' Cookbook: From Mac'n Cheese to Double Chocolate Chip Cookies–90 Recipes to Have Some Fingerlickin' Fun*. Adams Media Corporation, 2008.

Pillsbury. *Pillsbury Kids Cookbook: Food Fun For Boys And Girls*. Wiley, John & Sons, Incorporated, 2005.

Ray, Rachel. *Cooking Rocks Cookbook!: Rachel Ray's 30 Minute Meals for Kids*. National Book Network, 2004.

Rosenbaum, Stephanie. *Food Fun*. Simon & Schuster, 2006.

Taliaferro, Elizabeth. *Southern Living Kids Cookbook*. Oxmoor House, Incorporated, 2008.

Wilkes, Angela. *The Usborne First Cookbook*. EDC Publishing, 2007.

What Children Need to Learn to READ

Williams-Sonoma. *Kid's Cookbook: A Great Book for Kids Who Love to Cook.* Oxmoor House, Inc., 2002.

Zanzarella, Marianne. *Good Housekeeping Illustrated Children's Cookbook.* Sterling Publishing Company, Inc., 2004.

Children's Joke Books

Charney, Steve. *Kids' Kookiest Riddles.* Sterling, 2007.

Dahl, Michael. *The Everything Kid's Joke Book.* Adams Media, 2002.

Hills, Tad. *Knock Knock Who's There: My First Book of Knock Knock Jokes.* Little Simon, 2000.

Leno, Jay. *Jay Leno's How to Be the Funniest Kid in the Whole Wide World (Or Just in Your Class).* Simon and Schuster Children's Publishing, 2007.

Maestro, Marco. *What Do You Hear When the Cows Sing?: And Other Silly Riddles (I Can Read Book 1).* HarperCollins, 1997.

Mauterer, Erin. *Laugh Out Loud: Jokes and Riddles From Highlights For Children.* Boyds Mills Press, 2005.

McCarthy, Rebecca. *Waddle Lots of Laughs.* Penguin Group (USA), 2008. (Disney Club Penguin Series)

Meyers, Robert. *365 Knock Knock Jokes.* Sterling, 2006.

Namm, Diane. *Laugh-A-Long Readers: Laugh Out Loud Jokes.* Sterling, 2008.

Phillips, Bob. *Good Clean Knock Knock Jokes for Kids.* Harvest House Publishers, 2007.

Phillips, Bob. *Fabulous and Funny Clean Jokes for Kids.* Harvest House Publishers, 2004.

Phillips, Bob. *Over the Top Clean Jokes for Kids.* Harvest House Publishers, 2005.

Roven, Jeff. *500 Hilarious Jokes for Kids.* Signet, 1990.

CHILDREN'S READING WEBSITES

Reading Activity Websites

http://www.abcteach.com — This site is full of educational worksheets. It has alphabet flash cards, phonics, Dolch Sight Words, word scrambles, word searches, rebus (picture) stories, spelling, grammar, nursery rhymes, coloring pages, writing, word families, and more.

http://www.beginningreading.com — The phonics site has free worksheets for letters, sounds, phonics and flashcards.

http://www.ed.gov/Family/RWN/Activ97/begin.html — Offers reading activities for children from preschool through grade two.

http://www.fidella.com/trmg/ — This site has the full edition of the original "The Real Mother Goose" published in 1916. These are the classic nursery rhymes that we all grew up with and should be passed on to the next generation of children.

http://www.gardenofsong.com/ — Offers nursery rhymes, children's songs, holiday songs, folk songs, and a listing of other children's music websites. Each song lists the words to the song and has a button to click to hear the music.

http://www.jayzeebear.com — This site has some fun alphabet games.

http://www.kcls.org/kids/whattoread/booklists/ — Visit this site for kid's booklists categorized by age and category.

http://www.kiddonet.com/gb/flash/phonics/Intro.html — This site has a wonderful, interactive alphabet learning game.

http://www.kindersite.org — This site is for teachers, parents, and kids. It has games, songs, lullabies, and stories.

http://www.learningplanet.com — Go here for alphabet, reading, and phonics activities and printables. It also has many other subject area activities.

http://www.lil-fingers.com — You'll find storybooks for toddlers here, alphabet games, coloring pages and more.

http://www.literacycenter.net — Literacycenter.net has beginning reader activities in English, Spanish, German, and French. There are activities for letters, words, keyboard letters, and more.

http://www.pbskids.org — Find all of your child's favorite PBS shows and characters at this site. There are coloring sheets, games, videos, music, and more.

http://www.preschoolrainbow.org/preschool-rhymes.htm — A wonderful preschool learning site. It includes rhymes, finger plays, action rhymes, songs, and book lists.

http://www.readwritethink.org — This is a great resource site for teachers and parents put on by the NCTE—International Reading Association. It includes lesson plans, standards, web resources, and student materials and games.

http://www.scholastic.com — This website has sections for teachers, parents, and kids. It has games, stories, printables, videos, activities, booklists, tips, and a free e-newsletter.

http://www.smart-central.com — Go here for all of your old favorite songs and nursery rhymes. You will find the full text versions and can also print them out.

http://www.softschools.com/ — Softschools.com has alphabet coloring sheets, phonics worksheets, and printables in many other subject areas.

http://www.starfall.com — You'll find a plethora of wonderful reading activities here. Kids can work on their ABCs and letter sounds. They can read beginning reader stories, plays, comics, folk tales, etc.

http://www.storyplace.org — Storyplace.com has online stories with musical songs, activities and reading lists.

http://www.theschoolbell.com — This site has reading activities and the Dolch Sight Words. It also has reading and other subject area lesson plans.

http://www.yourchildlearns.com — Go here for online letter and phonics games and printables.

Online Reading Tests

http://www.longman.com/ae/marketing/sfesl — This site contains reading passages and questions to test students in grades 1 through 8.

Fun Birthday Cake Ideas (can be tied in with a book)

http://childparenting.about.com/cs/birthdayparties/a/birthday-cakes.htm

http://familyfun.go.com/recipes/special/specialfeature/cakefinder-birthday/

http://www.dltk-kids.com/crafts/birthday/cakes.html

http://www.kidsdomain.com/craft/_bd-cake.html

http://www.kidsturncentral.com/links/bdcakes.htm

What Children Need to Learn to READ

Parent & Teacher Resources

http://www.readingrockets.org — This site has reading resources/guides, techniques for teaching reading/helping struggling readers, books and authors, PBS shows, reading blogs, and webcasts.

Children's Reading Software

Bailey's Book House (Ages 3-7). Edmark

Blues Clues Preschool for PC (Ages 3-5). PC

Blues Clues Kindergarten (Ages 4-6). Humongous Entertainment

Caillou Ready for School. Brighter Minds

Clifford the Big Red Dog: Phonics (Ages 4-6). Scholastic

Curious George Preschool Learning Games (Ages 3-5). Simon & Schuster

Curious George Learns Phonics Kindergarten–1st Grade. Pearson Software

Disney's Winnie the Pooh: ABCs (Jewel Case) (Ages 3-6). Disney

Disney's Winnie the Pooh: Spelling (Jewel Case) (Ages 3-6). Disney

Dr. Seuss Toddler (Ages 1½-3). The Learning Company

Dr. Seuss ABC (Ages 3-7). The Learning Company

Dr. Seuss Cat in the Hat (Ages 3-7). The Learning Company

Dr. Seuss Green Eggs and Ham (Ages 3-7). The Learning Company

Dr. Seuss Reading Games (Ages 3-7). Creative Wonders

Mia's Reading Adventure: The Bugaboo Bugs. Kutoka Interactive, Inc.

Mia's Reading Adventure: The Search for Grandma's Remedy. Kutoka Interactive, Inc.

Reader Rabbit Playtime for Baby. The Learning Company

Reader Rabbit Playtime for Baby & Toddler (Ages 1-3). The Learning Company

Reader Rabbit Toddler. The Learning Company

Reader Rabbit Preschool Classic (Jewel Case) (Ages 3-5). The Learning Company

Reader Rabbit Preschool 2005 (Jewel Case) (Ages 3-5). The Learning Company

Reader Rabbit Learn to Read With Phonics (Ages 3-6). The Learning Company

Reader Rabbit Learn to Read With Phonics Preschool & Kindergarten (Ages 3-6). The Learning Company

Reader Rabbit Reading (Ages 4-6). The Learning Company

Reader Rabbit Kindergarten. The Learning Company

Reader Rabbit Kindergarten (Jewel Case) (Ages 4-6). The Learning Company

Reader Rabbit 1st Grade Classic Edition. The Learning Company

Reader Rabbit 1st Grade (Ages 5-7). The Learning Company

Reader Rabbit 1st Grade Capers on Cloud Nine (Ages 5-7). The Learning Company

Reader Rabbit I Can Read With Phonics! 1st & 2nd Grade (Ages 5-8). The Learning Company

Sesame Street First Steps (Ages 1½-3). Nova Development US

Sesame Street Let's Make a Word (Ages 3-6). Encore

Sesame Street Preschool (Ages 3-5). Nova Development US

Look at What I Read!

Reading Goals Sheet

Name _____

Date _____ Reading goal _____
1. _____
2. _____
3. _____
4. _____
5. _____
6. _____

Date _____ Reading goal _____
1. _____
2. _____
3. _____
4. _____
5. _____
6. _____

Date _____ Reading goal _____
1. _____
2. _____

3. _____
4. _____
5. _____
6. _____

Date _____ Reading goal _____
1. _____
2. _____
3. _____

What Children Need to Learn to READ

4. _____

5. _____

6. _____

Date _____ Reading goal _____

1. _____

2. _____

3. _____

4. _____

5. _____

6. _____

Date _____ Reading goal _____

1. _____

2. _____

3. _____

4. _____

5. _____

6. _____

Date _____ Reading goal _____

1. _____

2. _____

3. _____

4. _____

5. _____

6. _____

My favorite book was: _____

Why?_____

_____

My favorite character was: _____

Why?_____

_____

Look at What I Read! Reading Goals Sheet

195

My Reading Chart

Name _____

What Children Need to Learn to READ

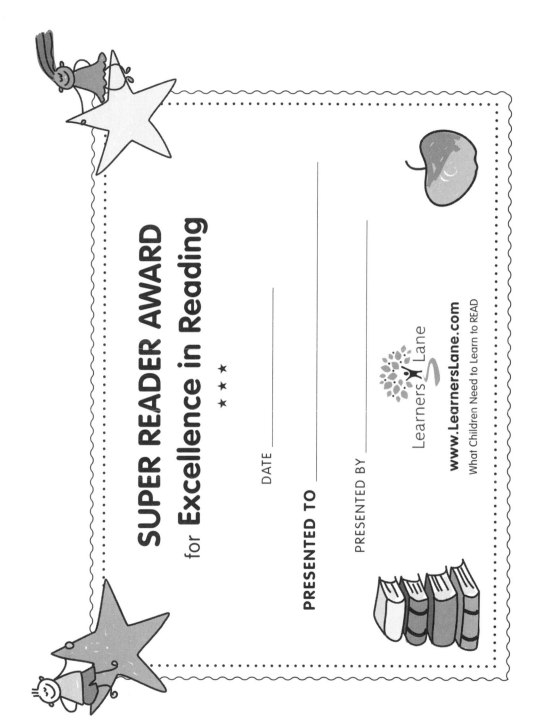

SUPER READER AWARD
for **Excellence in Reading**

★ ★ ★

DATE _____

PRESENTED TO

PRESENTED BY _____

Learners Lane

www.LearnersLane.com
What Children Need to Learn to READ

What Children Need to Learn to READ

Index

C

D

H

I

J

K

L

M

Q

R

Y

Z

About the Author

Michelle Vallene resides in Redmond, Washington, with her husband, Brian, and their three wonderful children, Briana, Brittany, and Kevin. She holds a teaching degree from Washington State University, with endorsements in English and reading. She was the Student State President of the Washington Education Association while in college. Michelle first started teaching at Salem Woods Elementary in Monroe, Washington, and now teaches part-time at Einstein Elementary in Redmond, Washington. When Michelle took time off to raise her children, she started a successful education company, Learners Lane, which specializes in after-school, and summer enrichment programs, as well as dynamic educational products. During this time, she worked to develop an unparalleled reading curriculum that she started teaching out of her home to groups of young children. The classes became so successful that she hired additional teachers to help her with the growing demand. The classes then moved out of her home and into local community centers where they still continue to help young children get a jump-start in learning to read. Suzie Connor, her good friend and business partner, has helped Michelle to shape the direction and vision of the company. Michelle and Suzie continue to be innovators in education, developing outstanding enrichment curriculum in the areas of math, creative writing, and chess, in addition to their successful reading programs. The two see the impact that education, teachers, and parents have on the future, and they continue to follow their vision to do their part in making the world a better place, one child at a time.

What Children Need to Learn to READ

www.LearnersLane.com

QUICK ORDER FORM

Email orders: info@LearnersLane.com

Postal orders: Learners Lane
PO Box 2303,
Redmond, WA 98073

Please send the following books, products. I understand that I may return any of them for a full refund, for any reason, no questions asked. _____

_____

_____

_____

_____

❏ **Please sign me up for your FREE educational newsletter via email**
(includes valuable study tips, great children's websites, upcoming classes, events, products and much more):

Email address: _____

❏ **Please send me FREE information** on having author, Michelle Vallene, come speak at your next group event.

Name: _____

Address: _____

City: _____ State: _____ Zip: _____

Telephone: _____

Email address: _____

Book Cost: $14.95 plus shipping and handling, and tax where applicable

Sales tax & Shipping: Please check www.LearnersLane.com for sales tax and shipping costs.

Payment: ❏ Check (please make payable to Learners Lane)

Credit card: ❏ Visa ❏ MasterCard ❏ Discover

Card number: _____ CVN _____

Name on card: _____ Exp. Date: _____

Learners Lane   www.LearnersLane.com